P

48 YEARS ON THE FOOTPLATE

48 YEARS ON THE FOOTPLATE
1942-90

ROLAND RUFFELL

• RAILWAY HERITAGE •
from
The NOSTALGIA Collection

First published in 2007
Reprinted 2007

British Library Cataloguing in Publication Data

A catalogue record for this book is available from the British Library.

ISBN 978 1 85794 288 0

Silver Link Publishing Ltd
The Trundle
Ringstead Road
Great Addington
Kettering
Northants NN14 4BW

Tel/Fax: 01536 330588
email: sales@nostalgiacollection.com
Website: www.nostalgiacollection.com

Printed and bound in the Czech Republic

Unless otherwise credited, all photographs are by the author.

Frontispiece In the summer of 1954 'A4' 'Pacific' No 60034 *Lord Faringdon* emerges from Gasworks Tunnel outside King's Cross with the 'Yorkshire Pullman'. Driver G. Tee of 'Top Shed' and his fireman, the author, look out from the cab. *Eric Treacy, author's collection*

Title page A young Fireman Roland Ruffell photographed by Eric Treacy at King's Cross in 1954. *Eric Treacy, author's collection*

Left Class 'N2' 0-6-2T No 9499, the regular engine of myself and my driver Sid Piggins, still in LNER livery at Holloway North in 1949.

Right Looking back along our train from the footplate of No 9499 on the up line at Bayford, between Hertford and Cuffley, in 1948.

CONTENTS

Almost 50 years on the footplate! Fireman Roland Ruffell looks from the cab of Class 'B1' No 61090 at Royston in 1950, and Driver Roland Ruffell (retired) is seen on Class 'K1' No 62005 at Grosmont on the North Yorkshire Moors Railway on 21 October 1999. *Both author*

INTRODUCTION

The 24th of August 1942 was a damp misty day when, at the age of 15½ years old, I took the 10-minute walk from my home to Hornsey locomotive depot, where I would be starting my railway career with the London & North Eastern Railway (LNER) as a engine cleaner, doing odd jobs and working on the 'J17', 'J52', 'N1' and 'N2' locomotives that were allocated to the depot at that period (to the best of my memory the 'J17s' were replaced by 'J6s' during 1943).

Hornsey was mainly a freight depot, but there were a few passenger workings in the King's Cross suburban area, worked by the 'N1' and 'N2' classes. There were also empty carriage workings in and out of King's Cross to various storage sidings, mainly at Holloway, Waterworks (Wood Green), Bounds Green and Hornsey. In addition, the majority of northbound freight trains started from Ferme Park Yards, worked by Hornsey crews to Hitchin, then New England crews forward to Peterborough. A varied assortment of locomotives worked these trains – 'J39' 0-6-0s, 'K2' and 'K3' 2-6-0s, 'O1', 'O2' and 'O4' 2-8-0s, 'V2' 2-6-2s and 'P1' 2-8-2s – while also at this period an LMS Class 8F 2-8-0 (No 8513) was shedded at New England, and worked its share.

A vast amount of freight was also worked from Ferme Park to the Southern Railway via the 'Widened Lines' (from King's Cross York Road to Farringdon, Snow Hill bank and across Blackfriars Bridge). These trains were worked by Classes 'N1' and 'J52', both being fitted with steam condensers for use when passing through the tunnels between King's Cross and Holborn Viaduct.

Other freight was worked by Class 'J52' 0-6-0 tank locomotives (which were non-condensing), serving the majority of the East London docks and routed via Finsbury Park, Canonbury and Stratford Low Level. There was also a great deal of local freight between various yards in the former Great Northern Railway (GN) suburban area.

On reporting to the cleaners' foreman I was given the job, with another cleaner, of cleaning only the numbers of engines based at Hornsey depot. We were later given a assortment of jobs to do, including the occasion when we were detailed to clean a Class 'J52' that had been altered to make it look like a German locomotive, as it was to be used in a wartime film. We were unable to find out anything about the film as it was all very 'hush-hush', as most things were during the war years.

Often a spare part would be wanted for one of the Class 'J17' 0-6-0s, so two of us cleaners would go to Stratford Works to get it, travelling by train from Palace Gates to Stratford via Seven Sisters. We used to enjoy these trips as it gave us the opportunity to visit the Works and see locomotives being stripped down and others in the process of being rebuilt. I can recall seeing a freshly painted ex-M&GN Class 'J93' 0-6-0T coming out of the paint shop in black with 'NE' on the tank; it had originally been built between 1873 and

A view of **Hornsey Loco on 23 June 1954.** *Alec G. Ramsdale*

1874 for the Cornwall Minerals Railway. At the same time a Class 'J92' 0-6-0 Crane Tank was doing departmental shunting at the 'Polygon', as part of Stratford Works was known.

There were ten of us engine cleaners based at Hornsey at this period, and we carried out various jobs, including filling sandboxes, clearing out the ashpits, assisting in the oil stores, issuing sets of locomotive tools and lamps, and generally helping to keep the running shed and loco yard tidy. During icy weather we helped keep the 'devils' (braziers) alight at the water columns, to stop them from freezing up. There were also visits to King's Cross 'Top Shed', and to Hatfield shed, to take or bring back a variety of items. We were therefore generally fully occupied, and all for a sum of £1 per week, with an additional 15-17 shillings per week for the heavier work.

The object of starting as a engine cleaner was to progress through the line of promotion to become a fireman and finally a driver, after passing the medical and technical examinations for each grade – this took many years to achieve, as promotion was very slow.

To further our knowledge of the steam locomotive, we would assist the drivers and firemen when they were preparing their engines prior to departing from the shed. Sometimes I would go with them for the experience. This would usually be on a Saturday and in our own time, and I gained a lot of knowledge from these unofficial trips between Ferme Park and Hitchin.

Most of us also attended 'Mutual Improvement Classes' to further our knowledge of the Rules & Regulations, and to learn in full the technical workings of the steam locomotive. Drivers and Inspectors gave their time free for this purpose, and of course we also attended in our own time. The LNER, and later British Railways, supplied the premises and working models of valves and pistons, and various other parts of the locomotive, together with technical books and diagrams. We had the occasional visit to Doncaster Works, which, thinking back now, was a wonderful experience, and something I will never forget.

Since it was wartime we were all issued with a military-style steel helmet and a Civil

Defence gas mask, which we were instructed to carry with us at all times. During a 1940/41 air-raid some bombs were dropped on Hornsey Loco, one bomb making a direct hit on a steam locomotive, another demolishing Hornsey station footbridge and blocking many of the tracks leading into Ferme Park Yards. I remember this incident very well, as I only lived a few minutes' walk away, and my friend's house was badly damaged by the blast.

Due to the shortage of firemen, the age for being passed as a Spare Fireman (Passed Cleaner) was reduced to 16½ years, so on 9 November 1943 I was passed by a Locomotive Inspector for firing duties. One condition was that, due to my age, by law I would not be allowed to work at nights, so we had a two-shift roster – 6am and 2pm every other week – which prevented youngsters working between the hours of 10pm and 6am. This changed when I became 18 years of age – then I would work round the 24-hour roster, which I was to do for the next 45½ years.

My first firing turn was with Driver Charlie Parrot on a Class 'J52', shunting in the Low Yard at Ferme Park on the afternoon shift. To this day I can recall looking out of the cab and watching main-line and suburban passenger trains as well as the many freight trains go by, many of the locomotives being ex-GNR 'Atlantics', and thinking to myself that perhaps one day I would be working on those jobs.

I enjoyed my first day out 'on the shovel' as a Spare Fireman, and working under Charlie's instructions I had no problems. Thus began my 13-year firing career, which over the years would take me across a large part of the LNER, later the Eastern and North Eastern Regions of British Railways; in addition I would work over much of the Southern Railway/Region, not forgetting some London lines of the LMS/London Midland Region. In addition, during my firing career I would work on 37 different classes of steam locomotives, which added a great deal of interest to the job. Each class of engine was a challenge as they all had their peculiarities. Indeed, no two engines of the same class performed the same. Though built to the same specification, they were all

My first firing turn was on an ex-GNR 'J52' 0-6-0ST, like this one photographed at Hornsey Loco in 1946.

At the Low Yard at Ferme Park I used to look out of the cab and watch main-line trains like the 'Flying Scotsman', seen here in 1948, imagining that I might one day work such jobs.

individuals – some steamed well, others were bad steamers, and this was where the fireman's skill came into its own.

Generally speaking a Spare Fireman booked on the shed could find himself cleaning fires, emptying smokeboxes, raking out ashpans, trimming coal, filling tanks and sandboxes – the list was endless. These were all very unpleasant and dirty jobs, but all done in the hope of perhaps one day becoming an engine driver.

Things did get better, however, and trips 'out on the road' become more frequent. I enjoyed going to the various places, but one snag was the 'blackout': all locomotives were fitted with blackout sheets to stop the glare of the fire escaping into the darkness, providing some form of protection against German bombers, as London was still getting some air-raids.

One of the worst experiences I had as a young fireman was working a train of petrol from Ferme Park to Romford on a Class 'J6' 0-6-0 during an air-raid, the cab covered in with the black sheets. We picked up a Stratford Pilotman at Channelsea Junction, and off we went to Romford, where we shunted our train into a siding, uncoupled, then proceeded to go light engine back to Hornsey Loco. I may add that we were really pleased to see the back of that train of petrol!

I was a Passed Cleaner for some 18 months without a rostered shift, sometimes working a different shift on a daily basis per week, so my social life was almost non-existent. This was why many people left the railway industry for work that had more sociable hours, and the likely reason why only three of us from the original ten cleaners did eventually become engine drivers.

As Passed Cleaners we were also loaned to other depots, on a weekly basis to Hatfield or King's Cross. I did not object to this system as it gave me the opportunity to get involved with another depot's work, working trains to destinations not covered by Hornsey depot. One of the snags of this system was working the full 8-hour shift at the other depot, to which daily travelling time had to be added; this involved working a 12-hour day as well as a seven-day week. When we complained we were simply told that there was a war on, and to think of the war effort. At this period we were only entitled to seven days holiday per year, and we worked most Bank Holidays, sometimes working both Christmas Day and Boxing Day – it was also very difficult to get a day's leave from work.

One occasion I remember well was when one of the driver's daughters was getting married, and he was refused leave to attend the wedding. He obviously did attend, and a freight train was cancelled – no driver. Why do I remember this so well? Because I was the fireman who was booked to work the train with him.

It was a case of too many trains and not enough crews to run them. A situation was reached when some staff were employed as firemen for shed duties only, not being allowed to go out on the road. They were classified as 'Not in the line of promotion', which meant that they would never become drivers due to their high age group (most were in their 50s) – they would be almost 65 years of age before they became a driver (it was taking about 15 years to get a driver's position at this period).

I have not yet mentioned the 'call-paper' system, whereby a card would be delivered by hand to a driver or fireman at home, telling him what time to report for duty on that day. This system was later abandoned and Post Office telegrams were used. To the best of my memory 8 hours' notice had to be given to a train crew, and the system could therefore be used to alter the on-duty time on the same day. It also applied to guards (and should not be confused with the older 'knocking-up' system of house calls). As can be imagined, this whole system was very unpopular for the disruption to family life that it caused.

During 1942 I joined the Associated Society of Locomotive Engineers and Firemen, remaining a member of the society for nearly 48 years; it was an organisation that gave me some valuable assistance and advice over many years.

Some time during 1944 I had to attend a medical at Whipps Cross for military service, and was informed at an interview following the medical that I would shortly be joining the Railway Operating Department section of the Royal Engineers. However, from that day I had no further communication from the military, and must presume that my railway service was too important for the war effort – I was never officially told that the military would not be calling me up. Later the railway industry was classified as a reserved occupation for certain grades. Due to rationing we were limited to the amount of food we could buy, but as we were classed as heavy workers we did get an extra cheese allowance.

Fireman R. Ruffell on the footplate of 'J6' 0-6-0 No 4239 in 1947.

1
FIRING AT HORNSEY

On 20 August 1945, after further technical and medical examinations, I was appointed a Regular Fireman, so now I would have a rostered shift with a Regular Driver in a 'link' (a set of footplate crews undertaking a particular series of duties). Over the years I would be able to progress from the lowest link to the highest, provided that I did not transfer away from Hornsey to another depot, something I was to do at a later date.

The Hornsey depot roster consisting of several links, which are listed here from memory:

1 Main line (mainly freight to Hitchin via Hatfield or Hertford North)
2 Passenger (suburban trains and empty carriage workings)
3 South London (freight workings to the Southern Railway)
4 North London (freight workings to the East London docks)
5 Yard pilots (shunting engines for Ferme Park Yards)
6 Shed and Spare (crew cover for link vacancies, shed work, holidays and sickness)

While working as a fireman at Hornsey I worked freight trains to various destinations, all of which started at Ferme Park and returned either to Clarence Yard (Finsbury Park) or Ferme Park. The destinations included:

- Hitchin via Hatfield or Hertford North, with the occasional trip to Peterborough
- Hither Green via London Bridge or Nunhead
- Feltham via Clapham Junction or Harringay Curve, Gospel Oak, Willesden High Level and Brentford
- Victoria (this would be with a Pilot Driver from the Southern)
- Herne Hill, Battersea, New Cross Gate and Bricklayers Arms (all via the 'Widened Lines')
- Mint Street (on the approach to Fenchurch Street)
- Poplar, Victoria, Millwall and West India docks
- Romford (via Channelsea Junction and Stratford)
- Acton, Wembley Park and Neasden Loco (via Harringay Curve and Gospel Oak)

Ferme Park itself consisted of a series of yards on both the east and west sides of the East Coast Main Line, with a double-track viaduct extending from Hornsey to Harringay and crossing all the main running lines so that wagons could be transferred between the various yards without interfering with main-line trains. These transfer trips would have a locomotive at each end, usually Class 'J52s'. The scrapping of these locomotives started towards the end of 1954, and eventually the 'J52s' and 'N1s' were replaced by 'J50s'.

Ferme Park Yards had four 24-hour shunting pilots, in addition to a further three or four pilots of 8-hour duration, which gives some idea of the vast number of wagons to be dealt with and marshalled into trains, mainly bound for the Southern.

At one period a proportion of the steam locomotives were to be converted from coal to oil-burning, and an oil refuelling plant was built (in 1947/48) between Hornsey depot and Hornsey Up Goods signal box, but I cannot recall it ever being used to refuel steam locomotives.

During my firing career at Hornsey I fired on many interesting locos working both freight and parcels trains between Ferme Park and Hitchin, including the following classes: 'A1' (before their conversion to 'A3'), 'A4', 'C1', 'D2', 'J39', 'K1' (the Thompson rebuild from the 'K4'), 'K2', 'K3', 'O1', 'O2', 'O4', 'V2', 'W1', 'P1', 'WD' 2-8-0, and LMS 8F No 8513 (which, as already mentioned, was allocated to New England depot for a short period). They were indeed a batch of very interesting locomotives, and when I think back it was great to have been able to work on them as a young fireman.

The trains were mainly of 65-75 wagons, all loose-coupled coal empties being worked to Hitchin, where we would be relieved by a New England crew who would work the train forward to Peterborough. At Hitchin we would brew a can of tea and eat our sandwiches, or pay a visit to the staff canteen where we could buy a meal – most depots had canteens during the war years. Then we would get instructions to walk about a quarter of a mile along the track north of Hitchin station to Cambridge Junction signal box, where we would then relieve a New England crew and work a train of 60-70 wagons of coal back to Ferme Park, still all loose-coupled; there were very few 'fitted' freights in those days ('fitted' meaning having a continuous brake system throughout the train).

One 8-hour-shift job was nicknamed the 'Crab & Winkle'. This was always worked by a Class 'J52', and shunted both Hornsey and Wood Green coal yards. It was always very popular because it was an 8am-4pm shift – in fact, a friend of mine who now lives in New Zealand was always changing turns so that he could work this job. I am still in touch with him and he still retains a great interest in railways to this day.

On one occasion, while shunting the yard at Palmers Green, a Class 'N2' failed on a Hertford North train in Palmers Green station. We took the failed engine off of the train, shunted it into the yard, worked the

Class 'J52' No 8829 in the Down Yard at Ferme Park waiting to depart with the 'Crab and Winkle' in May 1948.
Alec G. Ramsdale

train forward with our Class 'J6' to Hertford North, then worked the train back to King's Cross tender-first – this would be the only occasion that I would work a passenger train with a 'J6' 0-6-0.

There were a large number of workings to the London docks. In addition to the depot's booked trains, we often relieved on the Goods Road at Ferme Park, and frequently worked trains forward to Victoria Docks, where the sidings were adjacent to the warehouses and ships. When we worked to these docks for a full week, on arriving on a Monday we would only see the tops of the ships' funnels over the roof of the warehouses, but by the later part of the week all of the ships' superstructure would be in view over the roof, the vessels having risen due to being unloaded, something I had never thought about – it made me realise how low a ship must be in the water when fully loaded. I fired Class 'O4' locomotives on two occasions when working the through trains to Victoria Docks.

Thinking back to some of the experiences many of the drivers had during the London Blitz, one sticks in my memory. I was working at Poplar Docks, and while shunting in the yard with a Class 'J52' my driver told me about the day he was at Poplar when the German bombers set the London docks on fire. He joined others in a air-raid shelter while buildings were being blown up and anything that would burn was alight. When the raid subsided they came out of the shelter to find that the railway tracks out of the docks had all been destroyed, so they were instructed to drop the fire on their loco and make their way back to Hornsey depot, a task that proved to be very difficult due to the bombing. I thought to myself, here we are shunting in the same docks with the same class of loco, among derelict buildings with weeds growing everywhere some four or five years after the event – this must be firmly implanted in my driver's memory as if it was only yesterday, and I wondered what it might have done to his state of mind. Some 18 months later he was taken off the road with bad health, and worked in the stores issuing tools, oil, etc, to the train crews until he retired. In my opinion this was a result of the London Blitz, and no

doubt there were others who suffered in the same way.

On one of my many trips to Mint Street I recall seeing the famous *Cutty Sark* in the docks; it must have been one of her last sailings before she found a permanent home in dry dock at Greenwich in 1954. When working to Mint Street it was a great sight to see the trains coming out of Fenchurch Street hauled by the 4-4-2T 'Tilbury Tanks' and Stanier's three-cylinder 2-6-4Ts, these locos having been originally built for the London, Tilbury & Southend Railway. Sadly, by 1954 all the 'Tilbury Tanks' had been scrapped except No 80 *Thundersley*, which has been preserved.

The Port of London Authority had a very efficient self-contained railway system, which had some tank locomotives that were always in very good condition – the crews kept the interiors of the cabs spotless. We got on well with the PLA crews, often having a laugh and a joke with them.

All in all, I found working to the docks of great interest – there was always something different to see, with the added bonus of seeing the docks and ships at work, little realising that many years later London's docks would be closed. At least I did have the satisfaction of seeing them when they were fully operational. It was a sad sight when, in 1986, I travelled on a diesel unit from North Woolwich to Stratford Low Level and we passed what was left of Victoria Docks; where the sidings had been was completely overgrown with all of the tracks gone, but the warehouses beside the dock were still there. It was a very sad and depressing sight, a large chunk of London's history gone for ever.

One day a derailment on the Great Eastern line stopped freight trains from running to Temple Mills from East Anglia, and they were diverted through Cambridge and via Hitchin and Hertford North. There was a connection with Palace Gates just after passing Bowes Park, and they continued from there to Temple Mills via Seven Sisters and Tottenham South. I remember sitting in the messroom at Hornsey with my driver on that day; we had signed on duty 'Spare', so did not know what type of job we would get or where we would go. We received instructions to travel to Bowes Park, relieve on a coal train and, with a Pilotman from Palace Gates (my driver did not know the road) work it forward to Temple Mills, then take the engine – a Class 'K2' – to Stratford Loco. We then made our way back to our depot 'on the cushions', the end of another eventful day, and the only time that I would work a train over that section of line.

From Ferme Park there were some workings to Farringdon Market Yard, which was located at a lower level beside Farringdon (London Transport) station. These trips would be worked by a Class 'J52' loco fitted with condensers. It is so many years ago that my memory is hazy on the workings of the yard, but one thing I do recall is the importance of every train crew's favourite beverage – tea. The most important item carried by a driver and fireman was the tea-can, and when signing on duty the first question asked by the driver was 'Do you have a tea-can?' In addition, a good fireman always carried a spare 'gauge glass' complete with two washers; this had the dual purpose of proving useful should a gauge glass break in the cab (that is another story), but most important of all it was the ideal object for stirring the tea.

A job that was never very popular was the 'Snow Hill banker', which consisted of banking (assisting in the rear) trains destined for the Southern from Farringdon to Holborn Viaduct, then returning light engine to Farringdon for the process to start all over again. Between Farringdon station and the entrance to the tunnel where the climb up Snow Hill bank began there was a short siding with a water column where the tank could be replenished, the fire cleaned, and any light servicing that might be required carried out. In an 8-hour shift some 15 or 20 freight trains would be banked up this incline enclosed in a double-track tunnel.

The majority of these trains were from the 'Northern', but there were also many from the 'Midland', which would be hauled by a 'Jinty' 0-6-0T, some of which were fitted with condensing apparatus for working over the 'Widened Lines'. The banker would be a Class 'N1' loco, which always ran with the bunker facing south. There was a good reason for this: the object was to keep the exhaust from the chimney at the rear of the train so that it did not engulf the cab, bearing in mind that the line was in a tunnel where there would already be smoke from the leading engine. All in all it was a very unpleasant job, the shifts being shared by Hornsey and Kings Cross depots.

Locomotives working trains through to the Southern via the 'Widened Lines' always ran chimney-first when travelling south, so that the return journey would be made bunker first. Again, this was so that the exhaust was at the rear of the loco when coming up the steep rising gradient of the single-line 'Hotel Curve' tunnel between King's Cross (Metropolitan) and King's Cross Suburban station (platform 16). It was essential that the rear sanders were in perfect working order, should the loco start slipping, and the Curve had to be stormed at a reasonable speed to keep ahead of the loco's exhaust, hoping that the end of the tunnel would be reached before the cab was engulfed by smoke.

While on the subject of tunnels, spare a thought for the signalman who manned Holborn Viaduct Low Level Box, located in the Snow Hill bank tunnel, which was rarely free of smoke. At this period it was a Southern Railway box, but had formerly been a South Eastern & Chatham box.

Hornsey depot was allocated two jobs that were night shifts, and these were working fish trains from East Goods Yard to Clapham Junction, where a Southern engine would be waiting to work the train forward. These fish trains originated in Scotland, and would arrive behind a Class 'V2' loco. There were also fish trains from Grimsby to East Goods Yard, which would usually be hauled by a Class 'K3'. These trains were fast, with fully fitted vacuum brakes, and carried the No 1 speed head-code. Little did I realise that a few years later I would be firing on these trains when working them from Peterborough to East Goods Yard.

On the way to Battersea Yards on the Southern we frequently came to a stop at a signal prior to reaching the Yards, often stopping there for a considerable time. However, this was always of great interest to

The view from the footplate of an 'N1' between London Bridge and New Cross in 1945.

me because only a short distance away was Stuarts Lane loco depot, so I could sit there in the cab of my 'J52' and watch all the activity at a Southern main-line depot. You can't imagine how many different classes of locomotives I could see, bearing in mind this was between 1945 and 1948! Once again I little realised that one day it would all be gone, but at least I saw Stuarts Lane shed in all its glory.

Bricklayers Arms was one of the few yards to which I disliked working trains. Having stopped short of New Cross the train then had to be propelled back down a gradient, under bridges and round curves, then of course the process was reversed for the return trip. It was quite a hazardous operation with a loose-coupled train and in darkness; in fact, if my memory is correct, if there was dense fog (we had 'pea-soup' fogs in those days) these trains would be cancelled. A further hazard for train crews was that, having propelled the train up to the running lines, the red tail-lamp on our loco would have to be altered to a white before proceeding towards London Bridge; to do this you had to climb down on to the track, where there was the electrified 'third rail'. I was doing just this on a dark winter's evening when I heard a whistle and, glancing round, saw a train coming. I quickly wrapped my arms round the side-rod of my 'J52' as the express went by, still blowing its whistle – by sounding his whistle early, without doubt that driver saved my life. When I did get back into the cab it was a long time before I stopped

shaking, and it is something I shall never forget.

One memory of a trip to New Cross Gate was on a night shift just before Christmas with a Class 'N1' loco. We had worked a train of parcels vans there, and on arrival received instructions to wait for a train of box vans to work back to Clarence Yard. In the meantime it had started snowing heavily, and some 4 hours later we were still waiting for our box vans, which never did arrive due to point trouble caused by the snow. By now the snow was above the level of the rails, and was also affecting the electrified third rail, giving problems with the running of the electric trains. After a further long period the platelayers cleared the points of snow so that we could get out of the yard, so we finished by running light engine to Hornsey Loco and working excessive overtime. The only comment from my driver was, 'It'll pay for our nuts at Christmas.'

Although there were several workings to what was referred to as Herne Hill, it was in fact Brixton Yards, and to the best of my knowledge, having passed through Loughborough Junction, it was not much further before the Yards were reached. Being a short trip it was not unknown to do two of them for a day's work, but it would involve working some overtime.

As already mentioned, one of the first jobs a fireman did on reaching the destination was to go and brew a can of tea, either in the guards' room, shunters' bunk or signal box, where there would always be a kettle of boiling water on either a fire or gas-ring, depending on whether it was winter or summer. This happened all over the railway system, whether freight or passenger workings. I can remember one day going into the guards' room on our arrival at Brixton Sidings with my white 1-pint tea-can to brew the tea, and coming out with a 2½-pint dark blue one, having done a swap with a Southern fireman. My new acquisition was to give me many years of good service, travelling many thousands of miles on the footplate over much of the country. This was one of my happier memories of working a trip to Herne Hill.

While on the subject of working to the Southern, I must mention a trip on a Class 'N1' with a fish train with a maximum load from East Goods to Clapham Junction. Before leaving the yard we were informed that the Snow Hill banker had failed, and that we were to attempt to go up without the banker, being 'given the road' (clear signals) from Kings Cross Met through Farringdon and up Snow Hill. My driver agreed to take it on, saying that it was a challenge, but he was not very happy about Control saying that we would get a clear road – with so many signal boxes involved, many things could go wrong.

Once again it was a cold wet night and, having double-checked that our loco's sanders were working, off we went down through the tunnels to King's Cross (York Road) and entered the 'Hole', as it was called. We began the descent to King's Cross Met, and as promised we did have all green signals as we passed through the tunnels and up beneath what was known as the 'Grid Iron' into Farringdon station. With the track bearing round to the right, we began the climb up Snow Hill with a full head of steam – 175psi – and the regulator wide open. The smoke, steam and noise in the tunnel, bearing in mind that we were running chimney-first, was to be honest an experience that I would not recommend to anyone.

The end of the story is that we made it out of the tunnel at the Ludgate Hill end, but then stalled on the still rising gradient. I then had to carry out various Rules & Regulations and walk back to Holborn Low Level box to

protect the train. Eventually another 'N1' was sent from King's Cross station to assist us up the remaining section of the bank, and after a long delay we carried on to Clapham Junction. This incident took place over a Bank Holiday period, and our train, which had come from Aberdeen, was classed as a special; there were few freight trains running that night, and the engine that assisted us had been taken off of an empty carriage working as there was a shortage of locos due to the holiday period.

There were many workings to Hither Green, the longest route being via Nunhead, which involved some steep gradients. Most of us preferred the shorter and quicker route via London Bridge. Class 'N1' locos would again be used on these trains. I recall one very wet night when we slipping to a stop on the arrival road at Hither Green, caused by a greasy rail on a steep gradient with the sanders failing to work. It was an unpleasant walk in the dark, pouring with rain, as I made my way forward to find an assisting loco. This was the Yard Pilot, which to my interest was a Class 'Z' 0-8-0T. I then rode back on the loco, telling the driver exactly where we had stalled. On reaching our train I coupled up the assisting loco and off we went up into the yard. The 'Zs' were three-cylinder locos built in 1929 and designed by Maunsell; only eight were built. I watched these locos doing heavy shunting many times, and they appeared to perform very well.

When standing in these yards during daylight hours I clearly recall seeing 'Schools' and 'Battle of Britain' Class locos working the express trains. In fact, in early 1946 I took a photograph of No 21C64 *Fighter Command* from the cab of my 'N1'. From that date I made it a habit to always carry a camera in my bag while at work. At the end of the war it was difficult to get films, but I was able to get some records of the early days of my career.

'Over the South' was our term for the freight trains going to the Southern from Ferme Park, and all destinations were south of the Thames except Feltham, which is north of the river; we therefore had to cross the river twice to get there from Ferme Park, first by Blackfriars Bridge then by either Barnes or

'Over the South': a view from the footplate of a 'J6' approaching a signal stop at Hounslow in 1947.

'WD' 2-8-0 No 63118 in Feltham Yard, 1948.

Richmond Bridges. When routed via Richmond the Southern would provide a pilot driver, as Hornsey drivers did not 'know the road', but this route would only be used at weekends because of engineering work on the track.

Feltham was a large and busy marshalling yard and also had a loco depot. When we worked a train to Feltham via Harringay Curve, Gospel Oak, Willesden High Level and Brentford, we would go to the loco depot to turn our loco. This would avoid working our return trip tender-first, which could be very unpleasant in bad weather. Our locomotive would have been either a Class 'J6' 0-6-0 or a 'WD' 2-8-0. Sometimes there was a shortage of locos, and there were occasions

when I worked trains over this route with a non-condensing Class 'J52'. Due to the small water capacity of these locos' saddle tanks, we stopped at Brentford for water before finishing our trip to Feltham.

Halfway across Blackfriars Bridge (partially demolished in recent years) were some signals, and nine times out of ten we would be stopped at them. During the war years it was an unpleasant experience to stand there halfway across the Thames when a 'doodlebug' (flying bomb) came across with its engine running – if the engine stopped down it would come, and we hoped that it would not come our way, although we knew that somebody somewhere was going to get it. The blood runs cold to think what would

Crossing Blackfriars Bridge, 1945. The last 'V2' 'rocket' fell on Britain in March of that year.

have happened had the bridge been hit. Then we had the V2 rockets – no one knew they were coming until the explosion. Those were indeed very bad days.

After the war there were 'lock-in' periods during both the morning and evening rush-hours. This meant that we were impounded in the yards during the rush-hour, which could involve working more than a 12-hour shift. When you were single this was not very acceptable – in those days when you started a shift you did not know what time it would finish, so it was a problem to arrange any form of social life. I was often tempted to change my job, but it was my ambition to become a engine driver and the job was full of interest, which was why I stayed.

The Class 'J52' saddle tanks were one of the main workhorses at Hornsey, and there were two types. One type was fitted with condenser apparatus between the chimney and the dome, and these were nicknamed 'Starvers' – I have never been able to find out why. The other type had no condenser and they were mainly used on North London and London docks workings, much of this work running over the tracks of the former North London

Railway. The main jobs of the 'Starvers' were the South London workings, but they could also be utilised for local shunting, trip workings and empty stock workings to and from King's Cross. Looking back, the work that these locos did was remarkable for their size – to the best of my recollection the normal load would be 20 wagons of coal or 30 empties. Also, bear in mind that these trains were loose-coupled, and it was a art in itself to drive and control this type of train. The two main problems encountered were 'breaking loose' (couplings breaking) or injury to the guard by braking severely when the couplings were taunt. This was where road knowledge and experience, especially regarding gradients, was the sign of a good driver.

Firing to the 'J52s' was also an art that took time to master. With their restricted cab space it was not easy to fire, but after taking some skin off one's knuckles a few times it was not long before the skills crept in. One situation that did cause problems was when a large lump of coal blocked the bunker hole 'shovelling plate' into the cab; even extensive use of a coal-hammer could take time, especially if the coal grain was the wrong way, which would

Class 'J52' No 68757 at Ashburton Grove, Finsbury Park, in 1953.

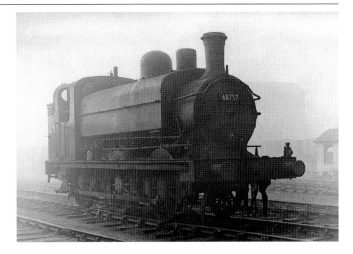

make it difficult to split; in the meantime boiler pressure and water level would begin to fall, then a battle would start between the fireman and the loco to build up both again. A good fireman would always have a supply of coal already broken up, but then down would come another big lump, and so it went on. Because the locos were coaled at a coal-hopper, there was no control over the size of the lumps falling into the bunker, and due to the small size of the bunkers this did create problems.

Climbing up on to the tank of a 'J52' to fill it with water, with the aid of one step and one handle, could be quite hazardous, especially when it was raining, snowing or blowing a gale, when it was not the best place to be! Precarious though it was on top of these tanks, I cannot recall hearing of anyone who slipped or fell off.

Another problem was cleaning the fire using a clinker shovel, when the handle would become very hot, but it would not be too long before a further skill was learned in the confined space of a 'J52' cab.

In my opinion and from the driver's point of view these locos were the ideal shunting engine. For instance, when a coal train of 60 or more wagons stopped on the 'Tango' arrival road at the Top Yard at Ferme Park, the shunter would halve the train so that our 'J52' would be pulling at least 30 of coal, on a slightly rising gradient up to the shunting spur, where the shunting would commence.

Having said that, one snag was that there was very little protection in the cab from driving rain or snow, so hooks were improvised on which to hang our raincoats in a attempt to keep the weather out; it would have been a good idea to leave the blackout sheets on the locos at the end of the war, but if my memory is correct they were all removed.

The first 'J52s' were built in 1897 and the last in 1909, and over the years they had various modifications done to them. When I was firing on them at Hornsey some of these faithful old locos were then more than 50 years old, and it says something for them that the last one was not withdrawn until 1961. It is good to know that one of the class has been preserved as part of the National Collection, and at the time of writing can still be seen in steam.

The other Hornsey workhorse was the Class 'N1' 0-6-2T. These locos were able to work virtually any job at the depot, being used for shunting at Hornsey Carriage Sidings, Bounds Green and Waterworks Sidings, and in addition, as already mentioned, they were used on freight, empty carriage workings and local passenger trains. All members of the class allocated to Hornsey were fitted with condenser apparatus, with a small minority having superheaters, and they were known by the crews as 'Small Mets'. On a shunting job they could prove hard work from a driver's point of view, due to having a screw rather than a lever reverser. Winding this backwards

One of the Hornsey workhorses, 'N1' No 69465, at Bow Junction in 1948. *Alec G. Ramsdale*

and forwards for a full shift really did do something for one's muscles! It was on many such jobs that the fireman, under the driver's supervision, was able to do half the driving for the shift.

One working I used to enjoy was to Hertford North, shunting en route the yards at Winchmore Hill, Crews Hill and Cuffley; on the return trip Bayford yard would be shunted (we are of course talking of a period when most stations had a freight yard, and a Station Master). Another job I used to enjoy was the New Barnet Shunt, shunting the yard at Oakleigh Park on the way.

As with the 'J52s', Hornsey had a large number of 'N1s' allocated to it, and they did a great deal of empty stock workings in and out of King's Cross. In fact, at the beginning of the film *Elizabethan Express* an 'N1' can be seen at King's Cross. Occasionally they could also be seen working a suburban passenger train in place of an 'N2'. I fired on a superheated 'N1' with a passenger train, and it proved to be a very good loco. Once again, by the time the last 'N1' was withdrawn they had been operating for 50 years.

Just a few Class 'N2' 0-6-2Ts were allocated

to Hornsey and were used for working passenger trains and empty carriage workings in the King's Cross suburban area, the vast majority being allocated to King's Cross (Top Shed). Some of the Hornsey 'N2s' had regular drivers and firemen, two shifts being worked on a few of them. Those with regular crews were very well looked after and maintained, and were known as 'Large Mets'. Their crews did their best to keep them clean, and inside the cab was spotless with all of the brasswork polished. They were a real pleasure to work on and to the best of my recollection they were free steaming, except No 9522, which for some unknown reason never did steam very well, and for obvious reasons never had a regular crew. This loco was painted in an 'apple green' livery after the war, as were several others of different classes – I believe this was done as a experiment.

The rolling-stock was two sets of four-coach articulated sets, some illuminated by gas, others by electricity. When hauling a 'gas set' it would be an easy trip as these sets ran freely, but it was a different story with an 'electric set', as the dynamos made the vehicles drag. To me as a young fireman this meant a harder

Working on the Hackney Wick Shunt, 1946.

trip, and when backing on to the train at King's Cross the first thing we looked for was the set's number, which would tell us whether it was 'gas' or 'electric'. Not all of the Hornsey-allocated 'N2s' were equipped with condenser apparatus, so those could not work over the 'Widened Lines'.

A few 'J6' Class 0-6-0s were allocated to Hornsey, and in addition to being used on the Feltham workings via the Harringay Curve, they were also used on turns doing local shunt jobs. These might involve picking up a train at Ferme Park, shunting the yard at Palmers

Green and the coal yard at Winchmore Hill, then on to the former Enfield terminus and yard (the station having been converted into a goods depot), diverging from the line to Cuffley and Hertford North at Grange Park.

The other main job was the New Southgate Shunt, which was a very busy working shunting both of the yards there, as well as the sidings of the Standard Telephone Company just south of Cemetery signal box. Both of these workings were two-shift jobs.

When the Hornsey breakdown crane and vans were sent out to any derailment, it was

Above A few Class 'N2' 0-6-2Ts were allocated to Hornsey to work passenger trains in the King's Cross suburban area. 'N2' No 9585 is at Hertford North in 1948.

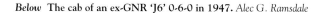

Below The cab of an ex-GNR 'J6' 0-6-0 in 1947. *Alec G. Ramsdale*

usually a 'J6' that would be working it. They were also used for snow clearance; in fact, one of my photographs shows a 'J6' fitted with a snow-plough. They were good all-round locos, but my main complaint would again be the GN cab, with no protection for the crew in bad weather conditions.

One Sunday afternoon we unexpectedly received instructions to make our way to Harringay to relieve a Hitchin crew on a ballast train working on the down main line, and to work the train forward to Hitchin. The interesting thing about this was that the loco was a Class 'D2' 4-4-0, which was the only time I worked on that class of loco.

The 'K2' Class 2-6-0s were known as 'Ragtimers', and as well as being used on freight they could also be used on passenger workings. I worked on several of the class, and my main memory was sitting on a piece of wood that was called a seat, with a Detroit lubricator bolted on the side of the cab in direct line with one's field of vision when looking ahead through the spectacle plate window (the purpose of this device was to lubricate the valves and cylinders). Also,

because it was worked by high steam pressure, it became very hot, and an added discomfort was again the GN cab.

While on the subject of the 'K2' Class, when on holiday in Scotland during 1950 I had the opportunity of riding on the footplate of No 61783 *Loch Sheil* from Fort William to Mallaig. This was a great experience and I shall always be grateful to the driver for the invitation. The Scottish 'K2s' were a little different from the ones I had worked on: first, they had side-window cabs, giving the crew more protection from the weather, which was no doubt much needed on the West Highland Line, and second there were 13 of them, all named after Scottish lochs.

The mainstay of the locomotives working freight trains down to Peterborough, a distance of just over 70 miles, were the 'Tango' 2-8-0s of Class 'O2' and 'O3'; the former had three cylinders and the latter two cylinders. They had a very long firebox, and it was hard work firing to them – it was a case of getting the angle right, firing through the flap and getting the coal down the front end under the brick arch. A fireman had to exercise a

Class 'K2' 2-6-0 No 61783 *Loch Sheil* at Fort William in 1950; I was lucky enough to ride on the footplate to Mallaig.

great deal of skill when firing to these locos. Being built for power, they only had small wheels so were not very fast, and working a train of 70 empty wagons through a single-line tunnel, with the loco being worked heavily, was not a desirable experience! I am referring to the down slow lines between Wood Green and Oakleigh Park, where two single-line tunnels were involved, both on rising gradients. We made sure that there was no smoke and no blowing off at the safety valves, and it was then a case of a handkerchief over the nose and mouth trying to breath. There were times when, due to the excessive heat from the chimney exhaust filling the cab, both driver and fireman would stand on the tender and lift up the tender flap, causing a current of cool air to rise between the engine and tender, making it easier to breath; as you can imagine, this was quite a precarious thing to do, but the older drivers thought nothing of it. When I think back it is a wonder that we have any lungs left! I know it was always a relief to come out of the tunnel, but I would immediately pick up the shovel and start firing, this being just part of the trip from Ferme Park to Hitchin.

By contrast, early in the morning just after the sun had risen on a beautiful summer day I can still visualise the scene when crossing Welwyn Viaduct, the low sun casting the shadow of our loco, the chimney-top exhaust, a full load of coal wagons and the viaduct arches. On this particular day our loco was a Class 'J39' and we had been stopped at Digswell at the south end of the viaduct; this meant that we were slowly accelerating towards Welwyn North, so we were able to admire not only the lovely view but also ourselves moving along the top of the viaduct's many arches, knowing that it would not be many minutes before we would be plunging into Welwyn South Tunnel.

The 'O2s' and 'O3s' were the original Great Northern locos, and a later version of the former was built by Gresley that did have side-window cabs. Later again, Thompson rebuilt some former Great Central Railway (GCR) Class 'O4' locos with new boilers and Walschaerts valve gear and reclassified them as Class 'O1'; these only had two cylinders.

While at Hornsey I fired on numerous locos of the 'K3' Class, including No 1863, which was a further Thompson rebuild from three to two cylinders; having worked on this loco when it had three cylinders, it was strange to hear the two-cylinder beat. I also fired on another of Thompson's rebuilds, No 61997 *MacCailin Mor*, which was reclassified 'K1', having been formerly a three-cylinder Class 'K4'; these locos all worked on the West Highland Line (Glasgow-Fort William-Mallaig). I had many trips on this loco and often thought of the days when it worked in Western Scotland – it was now a long way from its home territory. It was the forerunner of what became known as the 'Baby Bongos', but this class of loco was not one of my favourites to work on.

The 'K3s' were not very comfortable locos to work on, being rough riding. They had what we used to call a 'piano stool' for a seat; although padded it was more like sitting on a perch that wobbled with the vibration from the loco. They were nevertheless used on all types of train workings from slow goods to express passenger, and from the fireman's point of view they were fairly free steaming. They were known by train crews as 'Jazzers', and the nickname speaks for itself.

During my six years at Hornsey I only worked on a Class 'O4' twice. From a fireman's point of view they were not one of the best locos to fire – the shovelling plate on the tender was at a very low level, with the firebox door at a much higher level, so in my opinion it was not a comfortable firing position. However, apart from that they were good locos and whatever load they were given they would make easy work of it.

I was fortunate enough to have a small number of trips on both of the 'P1' Class 2-8-2 locos, Nos 2393 and 2394. They were known as the 'Boosters', although the 'booster' engines beneath the footplate had been removed many years before. These locos were originally built to haul 100-wagon coal trains, and were very powerful, although hard work for the fireman. They were the only locos I worked on that had a steam-operated reverser, and in my opinion they were fine-looking locomotives. I am glad that I did have a small number of trips on them before they were withdrawn from service during 1945.

I was also involved with the 'WD' 2-10-0 locos, but never actually went out on the road with one as a fireman – we would relieve the New England crew on arrival at Ferme Park, take the loco into Hornsey Loco and recondition it for the return journey while the crew had their meal break. This process would consist of coaling, turning, cleaning the fire and filling the tank, and my driver would oil it while at the same time looking for any defects. We would then take the loco light engine over to the Ferme Park Down Sidings, back it on to its train and get relieved by the New England crew. At this period these locos were all brand new and were khaki in colour. They were not on the Ferme Park workings for very long before they were transferred away; I think they all finished up going to Europe, helping to bring the war to a successful conclusion. It is nice to know that a few of these locos are preserved in this country, and are still running on our preserved railways.

The 'WD' 2-8-0 locos were liked by the majority of train crews. They were a comfortable loco to work on and very free steaming. Even with a 'dirty' fire (one with lots of clinker) they would still steam freely – in fact, I cannot recall ever being short of steam while working on these locos. They were powerful, could pull any load given to them, and could always be recognised when coasting by the clanking, which appeared to come from the slide bars.

The whistle on 'WD' locomotives had a very distinctive Midland sound, and they were equipped with vacuum, Westinghouse and steam brake systems when first built, but the Westinghouse system was removed after the war when these locos made their way back to the LNER and later British Railways.

A class of loco I never worked on was the American 2-8-0 'S160' Class, many of which worked between Temple Mills and March, so

The 'WD' 2-8-0s were generally popular, being a comfortable loco to work on and very free steaming. I am in the cab of No 63173 at Gospel Oak in 1948.

would be manned by Stratford and March crews. For some reason these locos were kept away from the 'Northern' metals between London and Peterborough.

During my six years at Hornsey depot I found the drivers and firemen to be a good lot to work with. Many of the drivers were real characters. One, Bill Smith, always smoked a clay pipe, and had overalls that were a shade of blue and always oil-free, although he always did all of his own oiling in the preparation of the loco. The majority of drivers expected the fireman to oil 'the underneath', and on a Class 'J52' or 'N1' this would involve climbing up between the eccentric rods to oil the big-ends and eccentrics; this section of the rods was then wiped clean by the person doing the oiling, so they were always clean. I hasten to add that this was the only part of the loco kept clean underneath.

To this day I can remember the names of the majority of the colleagues with whom I had the pleasure to work; sadly the drivers are no longer with us, but they will not be forgotten. Some of them encouraged their fireman to do the driving while working at the shed. This would be 'ashpit duties' – when the locos arrived back at the shed we would coal them, turn them if required, and fill the tank, then leave the engine on the ashpit for the fire to be cleaned.

Then there were 'shed setting duties', which involved moving the engine from the ashpit to the shed or a siding (the shed had eight tracks). This was sometimes a problem as the loco would be low in steam, and although a loco could be moved with low steam pressure, it was another story when you came to try and stop it with an inoperative vacuum brake due to the low pressure; it would be better with a steam brake, but at this period none of the locos allocated to Hornsey had those.

Opposite the entrance to the depot there was a small café that did a roaring trade, and I had many cups of tea and Chelsea buns there. A canteen was also provided for all railway staff working at the depot and Ferme Park Yards, as well as any other train crews working into the yards. Canteens were provided at most depots and yards throughout the whole

of the railway system, which I understand was a wartime measure.

Each depot had several messrooms – footplate staff, fitters and shedmen all had their own rooms, and each kept to their own, rarely mixing. The footplate staff messroom was known as the 'drivers' room' over the majority of the system. Most of these drivers' rooms took the same pattern: they tended to be austere with a large open fireplace, two tables running the full length of the room with bench-style seats, and shelves, also the length of the room, where the drivers and firemen kept their boxes. These would be specially made metal boxes painted black and locked with a small padlock. In the box would be tea-can, food for the shift, cup, cutlery, working timetables and various other official railway publications to do with a normal day's work. Most footplate staff also carried a couple of spare gauge glasses with washers, and some even carried a gauge glass spanner, although this would be part of the loco's normal tool equipment. The boxes measured approximately 10 inches by 14 inches, and were 10 inches deep. Left at the depot when you went home, they were privately purchased and were manufactured by 'J. Duke Ltd, Ironmongers, Grimsby'. The majority of footplate staff owned one, and this had been the practice for many years and was still so when I started my career in 1942.

Some time after 1950 most crews began to carry a government surplus shoulder-bag; in fact, I used a shoulder bag right up until British Railways issued train crews with an official leather driver's equipment bag.

Try and imagine that you are entering the drivers' room on a cold winter's day. There is a big coal fire (and I mean *big* – remember that there is a endless supply of coal) with an equally big kettle of boiling water. There might be a game of cards or dominos going on while meal breaks are being taken. There is a Victorian-style desk where the locomotive repairs book is located, and there are probably a couple of drivers checking the book to see if the locomotive they have been allocated has any defects and, if it has, whether the repair has been carried out – the fitter who has done the repair will have signed the book.

A Class 'J52' undergoing repairs at Hornsey in 1946. *Alec G. Ramsdale*

There is no daylight in the room; it is lit by high-wattage light bulbs, and there is one window that looks out into the running shed where, through the gloom, the locomotives can be seen. For obvious reasons this window is never opened. Drivers and firemen are chatting socially and discussing what sort of trip they have just done, whether the engine was a good steamer and where they had lots of signals against them, then someone offers a cup of tea so that will be another delay going home. Then, to round it all off, a daily driver's ticket will have to be filled in, giving full details of the day's work and accounting for every minute worked, a log of all trains worked, delays and loads, and part of it filled in by the guard. This has to be handed in to the timekeeper at the time of booking off duty. So as you can see it is not the glamorous job that people might like to think.

As regards the fireman's job, having prepared the engine and now ready to leave the shed, he would go to the drivers' room, wash some of the grime off his hands, then go to the kettle and make a brew of tea. This was very important as no engine left the shed without a can of freshly made tea, hence the reason why the aforementioned large kettle was always on the boil.

At a loco depot there were times when things could go badly wrong. At Hornsey there were occasions when, turning a Class 'V2' 2-6-2, the turntable stuck halfway round, which meant that the loco had to be moved about 12 inches to rebalance the table. To move a 'V2' that short distance and stop was not easy using a vacuum brake, and the driver moved the loco, could not stop, ran off the turntable and crashed into the wall of the General Office, knocking it down. The same thing happened a few months later, so some maintenance was then done to the turntable to make it balance correctly.

On another occasion I witnessed a Class 'N1' being driven along the ashpit when suddenly, without warning, the ashpit collapsed on one side, leaving the loco tilting over at 45 degrees. This shook up the driver – he was lucky not to get injured – and after this incident the ashpits were cleaned out more frequently, with the ashes and clinker removed, as it had been the continuous heat from the dropped fires that had made the walls of the pit collapse.

One afternoon I had just signed on duty when there was a almighty crash from the direction of the turntable. When we arrived on the scene there was a 'J52' in the well of the turntable, which was halfway round with a Class 'O2' 'Tango' on it in the process of being turned. I never did find out the cause of this accident, but I would imagine that the driver of the 'J52' had some explaining to do.

Now and again there was the odd derailment in the loco yard, but nothing serious, I am pleased to say. These larger incidents were spread over a period of years, so it was not all doom and gloom – in fact, most of the time everything ran smoothly. There was the odd occasion when the coal-hopper broke down, then the old-style coal stage would be brought back into service. It was hard work emptying the wagons by hand into large tubs, then wheeling them to the top of a short chute and tipping the coal either into the loco bunker or tender, this work being done by the staff who would normally be working the coal-hopper.

After nearly six years at Hornsey I was beginning to feel that I would like to transfer to King's Cross (Top Shed) and hopefully work on the main line. The only way I could do this was a mutual exchange with a Top Shed fireman, so I sent in an application and some weeks later had a reply to the effect that an exchange of depots with a Top Shed fireman was in the process of being arranged.

I hope this chapter has given some idea what it was like to work as a young fireman at Hornsey depot, and I did have mixed feelings when one day, after signing on duty, a letter was handed to me to say that five days later, on 23 August 1948, I was to report to Top Shed at 9am for duty. I had thus worked at Hornsey depot for a total of six years to the day.

2
TOP SHED AND THE 'MET' LINK

Travelling to and from work was to be a new experience for me, as in the past I had only lived a few minutes' walk away from the depot. The journey now involved travelling by train from Hornsey to King's Cross, in an eight-coach 'quad' set hauled by a Class 'N2' 0-6-2T (a 'quad' set was four articulated carriages mounted on five bogies, two sets being coupled together to make a train). On arrival at the terminus it would be a further 20 minutes' walk to Top Shed.

It was a strange feeling signing on duty for the first time at Top Shed. Almost everyone was a stranger to me, although I did have two uncles who worked in the workshops. The first person I had to see was Loco Inspector George Manyard, who explained to me the different sections of the loco yard, what they were called, their function and the general running of the shed.

Very soon I was teamed up with a driver for the rest of the day. My first job was to walk down to 'the Cross' and relieve on a train arriving from Edinburgh. The engine was a Class 'A4' 'Pacific' with a Top Shed crew who had worked to Grantham and back for their day's work, which would of course have included servicing their engine at Grantham Loco for the return trip. I had a feeling of satisfaction on stepping into the cab of the 'A4' as the fireman, and it was not long before the empty stock was hauled away to the carriage sidings. We then followed it down to the end of the platform and awaited the signal to 'give us the road' to take the engine to Top

Shed for turning and reconditioning, bringing to an end my first interesting day's work at Top Shed.

The railway promotion system worked on a seniority basis. On my transfer to Kings Cross I knew that for a start I would be rostered in the lowest 'link', then I would progress through the links as vacancies occurred in each until I reached my correct link position for my seniority, which would be the 'Regular Met Link'. By doing this no fireman would be displaced.

It was some months before I reached my proper link position, and progressing through the links involved an assortment of work:

- Shed and relief work
- Reconditioning and turning engines at King's Cross Passenger Loco
- Yard and local goods
- Snow Hill banker, Clapham Junction and Feltham
- Empty carriage workings
- Local passenger diagrams
- Freight workings to Edgware, Mill Hill East and High Barnet
- Finsbury Park to Alexandra Palace ('push and pull' diagrams)

Some of this work was new to me so I found it an interesting period. For example working a freight train from Highbury Vale Yard to any of the destinations beyond East Finchley was a challenge due to the continuous rising gradient from Finsbury Park No 1 signal box, then climbing through the stations at Finsbury Park, Stroud Green, Crouch End and Highgate (where there were two unpleasant single-line tunnels), then on to Park Junction (where the Alexandra Palace line branched off), and through East Finchley (where the track levelled out) to Finchley Central, running over London Transport's Northern Line.

Beyond Finchley Central the High Barnet line branched off to the right, then we passed through West Finchley, Woodside Park and Totteridge & Whetstone before arriving at High Barnet, the terminus of this section of the Northern Line. Here there was a yard that handled both coal and freight. There was only one working a day, the return trip going back to Highbury Vale with freight and empty coal wagons.

From Finchley Central there was also a line to Mill Hill East, where some of the Northern Line trains terminated; further on was the Mill Hill Gasworks, and the line eventually terminated at Edgware. To the best of my recollection there was also a daily working to Edgware, but without doubt the most important workings were the numerous coal trains bound for Mill Hill Gasworks. It was always a case of a full load of coal going and a full load of empties back to Highbury Vale. The shunt pilot at Highbury Vale was a Class 'J52', being kept busy from 6am until early evening.

It was a new experience for me working over the London Transport system, and at first it appeared strange that every train passed was a 'tube train'; viewing them from the footplate of an 'N2' I realised how low they were in comparison with our own stock.

Mention should be made about the driving skills required while working these loose-coupled trains over the London Transport system, bearing in mind that the only brake available was the vacuum brake on the loco, a handbrake and the guard's handbrake in his van; should the train begin to get out of control for some reason, the only way to get the guard's assistance was a continuous series of 'pop' whistles, on hearing which the guard would do his best by screwing on his handbrake to help bring the train under control. This would be an extreme measure

and I am pleased to say that I only experienced this situation once. The way that the drivers handled these trains, which were being run in 'paths' between the tube trains, was a education, and I was fortunate in gaining many of my skills from their knowledge.

Highbury Vale Yard was very near Arsenal (Piccadilly Line) underground station, and only a few minutes walk from the Arsenal football ground. In fact, when we shunted the yard on a Saturday afternoon when a match was in progress we always knew which team had scored a goal by the loudness of the roar from the spectators. Another function of the yard was the transfer of Northern Line stock used on the Finsbury Park to Moorgate service from the depot at Drayton Park to the Wellington Sidings, between Highgate and East Finchley, and vice versa. There was a tunnel that connected Highbury Vale Yard to the Northern Line tracks at Drayton Park, the empty stock being propelled to the yard by a London Transport battery locomotive, then a BR loco with a special coupler wagon attached would couple on and pull the tube stock into the yard. The stock would then be hauled to Wellington Sidings. The BR loco would either bring back any stock that had been overhauled, or return light engine.

Working on a 'push and pull' train was to be another new experience for me. This was the service operated between Finsbury Park and Alexandra Palace, which only ran in the peak hours of the rush-hour. During the period I was working on this service the locomotives used were ex-Great Central Class 'F2' 2-4-2Ts, and the three locomotives I recall firing on were Nos 5777, 5780 and 5783, built in 1896. Their load was two coaches, one of them being equipped with a driving cab; this meant that on the return journey from Alexandra Palace to Finsbury Park, the fireman was alone on the footplate while the driver was at the other end of the train, something that I found an odd experience. This must have been about the only occasion when a steam locomotive was working a train with only one man on the footplate, bearing in mind that the loco was propelling the train.

Nevertheless I enjoyed the experience of working over this interesting branch. The

Above London Transport's Drayton Park depot in 1948.

Below An 'N2' on a two-coach Finsbury Park-Alexandra Palace working in 1954, the year that the service was withdrawn. *Alec G. Ramsdale*

Above and left Alexandra Palace station in June 1954: services were withdrawn from 5 July. *Both Alec G. Ramsdale*

steepest gradient was 1 in 59, and I can remember the views from the viaduct near Muswell Hill. Soon after working my last trips over this branch the 'F2' tanks were replaced by ex-GNR Class 'C12' 4-4-2T locos, which were eventually themselves replaced by Class 'N2' 0-6-2T locos. The service was withdrawn in 1954, and so ended a little part of the railway system over which I had the privilege

of working; the section closed was from Park Junction through Cranley Gardens and Muswell Hill to Alexandra Palace; the other sections from Finsbury Park to Park Junction and beyond remained open for freight.

The Class 'F2' locos on which I worked were specially fitted for 'push-pull' working, and being ex-GC locos the firebox door was again located at a higher level, something I disliked since it produced what I felt was an uncomfortable firing position. Being a four-wheels-coupled loco, the 'F2s' were also prone to slipping, and many times on a wet or greasy rail we almost slipped to a standstill on some of the steeper gradients. Conversely, on the return trip from Alexandra Palace such rail conditions made it difficult to stop at some stations on the falling gradient; it was known for the wheels to lock, and the train would then simply slide along, eventually stopping at the far end of the platform. Bearing in mind that we were a two-coach train stopping at a platform built to hold about eight coaches, there would be black looks from the passengers who would have to walk nearly the full length of the platform!

Mixed up with these workings I was also diagrammed to work local passenger and empty carriage diagrams, and yard and local goods, and much of this work was the same as I had done when working at Hornsey depot. Some of the shunting pilots were different, being in the yards at King's Cross passenger station, King's Cross Goods Yard, East Goods Yard, Clarence Yard, Holloway Carriage Sidings, and Highbury Vale Yard. This was of course a great opportunity for me to learn all of the local workings in the King's Cross and Finsbury Park areas, which even today is a very complicated network. Many of the places appeared easy to learn during daylight, but it was a very different story when it was dark or thick fog, and it took time to feel completely confident. All of this work was done on Class 'J52' locos – and when Patrick Stirling designed them he did not consider the comfort of the enginemen who had to work on them...

Another job new to me was reconditioning locos at King's Cross Passenger Loco. This consisted of relieving mainly Doncaster, Grantham or Peterborough crews, waiting for the empty stock to go off to the sidings, then taking the engine into the Passenger Loco, where the fireman would clean the fire (take the clinker out of the firebox), add coal to the tender from the small mechanically operated coaling plant, top up the tender with water, then move the loco back on to the turntable. After being turned it would then be moved into a siding to wait for its next working, the fire having been partially made up ready for the crew. While all of this was going on the driver would be oiling the loco and checking it for any defects, in addition to moving it while in the yard. As can be appreciated, it was hard work, and teamwork was essential between the driver and fireman.

When a loco had worked into 'the Cross' from York, Leeds or Newcastle, or an 'A4' from the non-stop Edinburgh to King's Cross service that ran during the summer months, it would be normal practice for it to be fully serviced at Top Shed.

A photograph from the footplate of 'N2' No 9499 at Clarence Yard.

In addition to the main-line engines using the Passenger Loco, it was also used by a large number of Class 'N2' locos, these being used to operate the suburban service and being allocated between the three depots of King's Cross, Hornsey and Hatfield. The pattern of servicing was very similar to what I have just described, except that the work was included in the train working diagram, so the loco was serviced by its crew between working passenger trains and empty coaches.

I also found myself once again working on the Snow Hill banker, working freight trains to Clapham Junction and Feltham, as Top Shed worked a few of these turns.

Working on the shed involved a variety of different jobs. Some days would be spent coaling locos and running them round to the ashpit ready for the fire-droppers to clean the fires, rake out the ashpan and empty the smokebox of ashes – not the best of jobs when the wind was blowing in the wrong direction. Sometimes a 'passed cleaner' or a fireman would be given this job to do, although I should explain that most depots employed 'fire-droppers', which was the only work that they would be doing.

Another job would be moving the locos from the ashpit to the sheds or the extensive loco yard. Very often the loco's steam pressure would be too low, due to the fire having been cleaned, to move it under its own steam, so the Loco Pilot, which would be a Class 'J52', would be coupled on to move it to either the shed or the yard, where it would wait for a crew to prepare it for its next turn, or if it needed some minor repair to be carried out.

Finally we come to another part of shed work. After signing on duty 'as required', both driver and fireman would report to the Shed Foreman for instructions, which could consist of disposal or preparation of locos, disposal (cleaning the fire, etc) having already been described. The most usual instruction would be to prepare a loco, and it probably would be an 'A1', 'A2', 'A3', 'A4' or 'V2'. The normal preparation time allowance for these classes of locos would be an hour, but depending on circumstances it could take longer. I will explain what was involved from the fireman's point of view.

Having established where the loco was located, the first place to visit was the stores, where the following kit of tools would be obtained, being the standard issue for every loco: head-lamps, gauge glass lamp, bucket, three spanners (including what was called a monkey wrench), handbrush, firing shovel, coal hammer, flare lamps (to provide illumination when preparing or examining a loco), two red flags and 12 detonators. The driver would be responsible for the two types of oil required and the oil feeder.

On getting into the cab, the first check was the water level in the boiler and the steam pressure, then you looked into the firebox to check the lead plugs, tubes ends and stays for leaks, and also that the brick arch was in good condition. While still in the cab you checked for the three fire-irons – clinker shovel, pricker and bent dart – and for a spare firing shovel (in case the one in use should break out on the road). Additional items to be checked were, on 'A1s' and 'A2s', the rocker grate key; on 'A3s' and 'V2s' the drop grate key; and on 'A4s' the handle to wind up the casing enclosing the smokebox door (the 'cod's mouth') and the drop grate key. On an 'A4' corridor tender you had to check that the screw coupling was in place, in case it was required instead of the buck-eye coupling, and on all locomotives fitted with water scoops that the scoop was in working order.

Should the steam pressure be low, it had to be raised to a reasonable level. The injectors had to be checked and in working order, and the smokebox door had to be opened to examine the tubes for leaks and to make sure that everything was in order. On closing the smokebox door you checked that it was airtight. The tender should be topped up with water, and the coal trimmed to make it safe so that none would fall off. You checked that a deflector scoop was fitted in the firebox door, and that the head-lamps were lit at all times due to tunnels.

The driver's duties when preparing a locomotive will be covered later.

Having now worked on an assortment of the jobs I have just described over a period of five months, the only thing I did not manage was to fire on a Class 'C12'.

Sid Piggins was my driver on Class 'N2' No 9499 in 1949, which still retained its number and 'LNER' on the side tanks.

I now found myself restored in my correct 'link' position, the 'Regular Met Link'. Sid Piggins was my driver on Class 'N2' No 9499, which still retained its number and 'LNER' on the side tanks; the number was also still on the buffer-beam, so I was involved with a little bit of railway history. Everyone in this link had a regular engine, which meant that there were two regular crews per engine, working early and late shifts every other week; this also meant that the majority of the locos would be at their home depot, Top Shed, at night.

At this time – 1948-49 – there were just under 60 Class 'N2' locos at the depot, and those not allocated to regular crews were booked on diagrams not in the 'Regular Met', but if for some reason our engine was 'stopped' (for a boiler washout, repairs, etc) we would be booked any spare 'N2' that was available. The system worked well, and it was very rare that we did not have our regular engine. The crews looked after their engines – all the brass and copper was spotless and any small jobs were done, while repairs booked by the driver were done before the loco went out on its next shift.

Tools, etc, were kept locked in the cupboard, and the fire-irons on top of the side tank were secured by a chain and padlocks, so when the loco returned to the shed the only item to be handed in at the stores were the keys, attached to a metal label with the loco number stamped on it. This system had two advantages: all tools were kept in first-class condition, and they did not have to be returned to the stores by the fireman.

My first week in the 'Met' link was an afternoon shift. After signing on duty, Sid and I walked down to Platform 14 at King's Cross Suburban, where an eight-car 'quad' set was coupled to No 9499 ready to leave 'all stations' to Hertford North. We relieved our opposite mates, then some 10 minutes later we got 'right away' and were off. No 9499 was right-hand drive, making it easier for firing as I am right-handed; some of the 'N2s' were left-hand drive, and because of the limited cab space the loco had to be fired left-handed. Personally I could fire both left and right, which did make firing that much easier.

We had an excellent trip to Hertford North and back, but to complete our day's work we still had a further trip to Welwyn Garden City and another to Hertford North. In between working these trains there was tank-filling, altering the head-codes and destination boards, and, if necessary, cleaning the fire, not forgetting making the tea and eating our snack. At the end of the day, as we were the late shift, we would go light engine to Top Shed, where we would book off duty.

My driver Sid turned out to be a good mate and engineman. He had started his career at Boston in Lincolnshire, and after cleaning and firing he became a Passed Fireman and transferred to King's Cross for a driver's position, where he stayed until retirement. In fact, he only lived 20 minutes' walk away from my home at Hornsey, and invited me to his house, introducing me to his wife and family. It was in Sid's house that I saw my first working television. We got on well together both on and off the footplate.

Considering that No 9499 was due for the 'Plant' (to be overhauled), she rode very smoothly, the valves and pistons were set to perfection, and she was also a very good steamer. In fact, all I had to do was show her the shovel and the steam pressure gauge needle stayed on 170psi.

After a couple of months we signed on one morning and Sid suggested to me that I should do the oiling – in fact, all of the driver's duties for the preparation of the engine – and he would do all my fireman's duties. When I returned to the engine after making the tea, Sid was sitting in my seat.

'It's your turn to do all the driving today, Roland,' says he. 'I'll do all the firing. It will help to keep me fit, and I'm a wizard on the blade!'

So I spent my first day on the other side of the footplate, which is a totally different feeling from being on the fireman's side of the loco. This was to be the first of many days doing this, and I would say that I was fortunate in doing some 40% of the driving while rostered with Sid as my regular driver. Although I did know the road, a great deal more knowledge came to me thanks to Sid – both firing and driving over a road is the perfect way to learn it.

It was the practice that all 'N2s' ran 'chimney north', so running back to King's Cross they would be bunker-first. The worst aspect of this was coming out of Moorgate, as this meant coming up 'Hotel Curve' into platform 16 at 'the Cross' chimney-first. The steam, heat and noise was horrific – it was a case of handkerchief over nose and mouth to breathe, and once again it was essential that the sanders were in working order, should the loco start slipping.

Platform 16 was also a bad place to start a

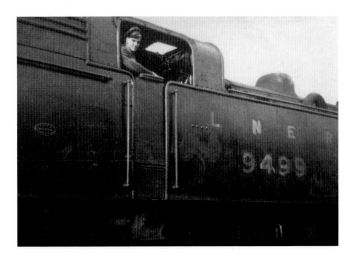

Myself on the footplate of No 9499 in 1949.

The 'beaver-tail' Observation Car of the 'Coronation' train, photographed from a moving loco in Hornsey Carriage Sidings.

train. It was on a curve and a rising gradient, the last coach being just outside the tunnel – and inside the tunnel were trap points, the object of which was to derail the train should it roll back too far, so there could be very little error when starting away. Sometimes on a wet day, when the rails were greasy and the engine kept slipping, another 'N2' would be attached to the front, and the train would go double-headed to Finsbury Park, where the assisting engine would be detached. All the time I was in the 'Met' link this happened to me only twice, and on both occasions we were working on a spare 'N2', not our regular No 9499.

Another occasion when it could be difficult to start was when the loco stopped 'dead-centre'. Without getting too technical, this was all about the position of the valves, and to move the loco it would need to be put into reverse, then, when it started to move, it had to be quickly reversed back to the direction of travel.

The suburban service was 'all go' and hard work. It was surprising how many station stops were made while doing three round trips – on average the total came to between 76 and 84, which included running into Moorgate and Broad Street.

Some of the diagrams involved empty stock workings, and very often we would work 14 or 15 coaches out of 'the Cross' to either Bounds Green or Hornsey Carriage Sidings single-handed. There was the odd time when a train of stock would stall going over the flyover between Wood Green and Bowes Park, and if this happened an engine would come out of

Waterworks Sidings to bank the stalled train over.

The procedure with these empty coach workings to Hornsey Carriage Sidings was that every train would be washed at Bounds Green, where the mechanical washer plant was located. After going over the flyover at Wood Green we would coast down and stop at Bowes Park station. The 15 coaches would then be propelled into the sidings at Bounds Green, then the loco would run round the train and propel it through the washer. We would then draw it back, giving it a double wash, then carry on to Hornsey Carriage Sidings with a fully washed train. I must say that a full-length train of teak-panelled stock after having been washed was a great sight.

One diagram I enjoyed working started at Western Sidings (Finsbury Park), then ran 'all stations' to Hertford North, where we ran round our train. Then it was off to Welwyn Garden City, calling at Hertingfordbury and Cole Green. We then carried on to Moorgate, calling at Hatfield and all stations, eventually running as empty stock back to Western Sidings, where we had our meal break before completing the rest of the diagram. The thing I liked about this diagram was running north on the Hertford branch, going over the single line to Welwyn and returning south via the GN main line. This, of course, will never be able to be done again, as the passenger service was withdrawn in 1951, and the track has all been lifted between Hertford North and Welwyn Garden City. A further interesting feature on the Hertford branch is Ponsbourne

The view ahead between Hertingfordbury and Cole Green from the footplate of No 9585 in 1948.

Tunnel, which is 2,684 yards in length, has five ventilation shafts and is the longest tunnel on the former GNR. During the hot summer months it was a pleasure to pass through it, as it was always cool and smoke-free, due to the ventilation shafts.

After some months No 9499 went off to Doncaster 'Plant' for its major overhaul, and we were allocated another 'N2', No 69549, which had 'BRITISH RAILWAYS' on the side tanks, with the number on the bunker. This loco was also right-hand drive, and would be our regular engine until 9499 came back from the 'Plant'. The replacement appeared to be a good engine and worked everything that was required without any problems.

While our regular engine, No 9499, was being overhauled at Doncaster, we were allocated No 69549, which was in the new British Railways livery. It is seen at Waterworks Sidings, Wood Green, in 1949.

That is until one day going down between Bayford and Hertford, coasting at just over 60mph on a dry rail, for no apparent reason the loco started slipping (remember that the regulator was closed and we were coasting). The reverser was put into full forward position and the cylinder cocks opened. The engine was vibrating so much that dust was coming up into the cab from the ashpan. The brake was fully applied, and when the speed dropped to about 45mph the slipping stopped. Neither Sid nor I had ever experienced anything like it before; it was reported and the engine was inspected on our return to the shed to try and find the defect.

The next day when we signed on duty we were informed that a loco inspector and the mechanical foreman would be riding with us on No 69549, so off we went to Hertford working the same train as the previous day, and exactly the same thing happened again in about the same place. On arrival at Hertford they immediately took the engine out of service, and we returned to the shed, where the loco was eventually placed in the workshops for a closer examination.

In the meantime we had a selection of the engines that were 'common users' each day. Some were good, some bad, and every day was a challenge, making it hard work. Not having a regular engine is a bad policy, and although Sid did his best to get another regular until No 9499 came back from the 'Plant', it was without success.

No 69549 spent a few days in the workshops, and on going back into service was booked out on empty carriage diagrams. To the best of my knowledge she eventually failed in Waterworks Carriage Sidings with a fractured big end (very unusual, and something I have never heard of before or since) – it was usually the brasses that were defective. Both Sid and I considered that we had been very lucky that this had not happened on the road running down to Hertford – the blood runs cold thinking about the consequences.

To our great surprise, one day when we looked at the list to see which engine was allocated to us for our diagram it was Class 'N7' No 69690. On checking I found that it

had a 34A (King's Cross) shed-code on the smokebox door, so this was to be our engine for the day, and a new experience for me as I had never worked on an 'N7' before. Hatfield depot had an allocation of about ten 'N7s' at this period, the shed-code being 34C, and this is where I thought No 69690 had come from, but I was wrong – it had been allocated to Neasden depot, 34E.

I enjoyed my day's work on the 'N7' – it was a comfortable engine to work on, and the cab appeared more spacious than an 'N2', which was probably because all the floor-boarding was on one level. The 'N2' was not like that – the driver's and fireman's sides were at a higher level than the central part of the cab flooring where the fireman stood to do the firing, which restricted the amount of space available. Having been brought up on 'N2s' this never bothered me, but I was friendly with a few of the firemen who worked at Stratford depot, and they did not like the 'N2' Class for that reason – they said all day was spent stepping up and down.

One of the things that impressed me about the 'N7' was its very rapid acceleration. No doubt this was due to the 4ft 10in-diameter wheels, compared with the 5ft 8in of the 'N2'.

The next unusual loco to be seen at Top Shed was a Class 'A5', an ex-GC 4-6-2T. This was a large engine, and if my memory is correct it was used only on empty coach workings – I have no recollection of seeing it on any passenger trains. Unfortunately the opportunity did not come my way to do any firing on this loco.

Sometimes a day comes along when one has a mental upset, and on one such day we were working a train from King's Cross to Welwyn Garden City, not stopping at Harringay and Hornsey, as was usual with many of these suburban trains. On departing from Finsbury Park we were turned out on to the main line, which was unusual, and meant that we would be turned from main to slow at the south end of Wood Green station to bring us into the platform.

Our engine being right-hand drive meant I was on the left-hand side of the cab, and we had just passed through Hornsey station when I saw a small group of platelayers standing

Above When No 69549 failed we were allocated Class 'N7' No 69690, a class that I had never worked on before. The loco is seen at Holloway North in 1949.

Below Little and large: unusual locos photographed at Top Shed in 1948. On the left is Sentinel Class 'Y4' No 8175, and beyond is Class 'W1' 4-6-4 No 60700, the former Gresley 'Hush Hush' high-pressure loco No 10000.

between the Nos 1 and 2 slow tracks, and I suddenly realised there was a fatality lying on No 2 slow track. This was the first time I had experienced anything like that – it was a shock to my system, and I found that for the rest of the day I could not dismiss it from my thoughts. That had been the reason for running us out main line at Finsbury Park. I must say it would have helped if we had been warned what to expect before departing from Finsbury Park, as the accident had obviously happened some time earlier.

A more pleasant experience was a social day out with a friend who was also a railway enthusiast. We had decided to have a ride out on the Metropolitan Line from Baker Street to Rickmansworth, and on our arrival at Baker Street we found in the platform a train of loco-hauled stock, teak in colour with slam doors, and coupled on at its head was a Metropolitan electric loco. These were of great interest, having been built in the early 1920s. There were 20 of them, and all had names; the last was withdrawn during 1961, and *Sarah Siddons* is the only one that was preserved, hauling occasional enthusiasts' specials. We chatted to the driver, and when he realised that I was on the footplate and my friend worked on London Transport in the signal maintenance department, he invited us into the cab, and we had an unofficial cab ride to Rickmansworth, which proved to be an interesting experience. It was my first ride in the cab of an electric locomotive, it was something that I was never able to repeat, but thanks to that driver we had a memorable trip.

Back on the GN, our regular loco eventually returned from the 'Plant' in all her glory, now numbered 69499, painted black and lined out, and with the 'starved lion' BR

crest on the side tanks. She was, I think, the first 'N2' allocated to 'the Cross' to come back from the 'Plant' in the new livery. We climbed into the cab as the fitters made a hasty exit down the other side. What had they been up to? Looking around, we saw that a black plate had been screwed on the inside of the driver's side of the cab, and painted on it in white letters was 'DRIVER S. PIGGINS. No 1 MET DRIVER'. As you probably realise, Sid got on well with the fitters, and this was one example of the things they used to do.

The months continued to go by and we began to find ourselves getting towards the top of the link, which meant that we would probably be split up when we moved up to the next link, which was the 'Odd Main Line', working trains to Peterborough and Cambridge.

By chance, at one of the model railway exhibitions held in London, I met up with Jim Maxwell, who lived at Newton Abbot and was the owner of a live-steam Armstrong 0-6-0 goods loco with double frames, taking it to railway exhibitions and private outdoor tracks. For some years I spent much of my leisure time driving this loco at various shows, but the track that has always stuck in my mind was the one at Thames Ditton, where on an open day I drove the loco round the track with about eight children behind me. On retirement Jim Maxwell spent a great deal of time on the Ffestiniog Railway. Another

When our regular loco returned from the 'Plant' it was in full BR black lined-out livery, numbered 69499 and with the 'starved lion' BR crest on the side tanks.

Above Driver Jim Maxwell and Fireman Alec Ramsdale with the former's live-steam model Armstrong double-framed 0-6-0 goods loco in 1948.

Below When he retired Jim spent a great deal of time driving on the Ffestiniog Railway. He is seen with *Prince* in September 1957.

Sid Piggins and I were now working into Broad Street with No 69499. This footplate view was taken between Broad Street and Dalston Junction in 1949; note the electrified lines on the left.

friend of mine, Alec Ramsdale, also a railway enthusiast and a fireman at Hornsey depot, shared the driving with me; many years later he and his family went to live in New Zealand.

In the meantime I was still firing on No 69499 with Sid Piggins, working our way through the roster and now finding ourselves running into Broad Street. After leaving Finsbury Park there were only two intermediate stops, Canonbury and Dalston Junction, then next stop Broad Street, which at this period was a very busy station. After our stock had gone, we would draw down to the end of the platform and go into a shunt spur, where the loco's tank would be topped up. This was an interesting location to stop for a few minutes as it overlooked Liverpool Street station, and provided a 'bird's eye' view of the 'Jazz' suburban service in operation, with trains going to Chingford, Enfield Town, Hertford East and Bishops Stortford. The main type of loco used appeared to be the 'N7'. It was a very intensive service with lots of engine movements taking place.

Meanwhile another train had run into the platform we had vacated, and, moving our loco out of the spur, we coupled on to our eight-car set and it would not be very long before we were once again heading for Welwyn Garden City, where we ran round the train, crossed over from the down to the up platform, and off we went to King's Cross.

After doing this type of routine on the 'Met' for well over a year, I felt that it would be good to be promoted up to the main line (bearing in mind that some drivers and firemen were doing this 'Met' work for years). Having now got nearly eight years' service completed, and having over those years worked on a varied assortment of jobs, I had gained a considerable amount of knowledge, and was now one of the senior firemen in the link.

A few weeks later my driver Sid was booked to 'learn the road' to both Cambridge and Peterborough, which included the whole of the New England loco depot, and marshalling yards. This would take him many weeks to learn, so in the meantime I was still working

My father, Fireman F. W. Ruffell, started at Top Shed in the mid-1920s and ended his footplate career in the early 1950s. He was involved in the Locomotive Exchanges of 1948, and is seen here with Driver T. Ratley beside Class 'B1' No 61251 *Oliver Bury* having run from Bristol to Plymouth on 30 June.

the 'Met' diagrams with different drivers, but on a weekly basis, though still with my regular engine No 69499.

The weeks went by heading towards May, and when the new rosters were posted for the following week I found myself rostered in the 'Odd Main Line' link, with Sid Piggins as my driver. It was very unusual for a driver and fireman to be moved up to a higher link and remain rostered together, but we were both surprised and pleased that we would still be working together as mates on the main line. While Sid continued to 'learn the road', I made my farewells to No 69499, working with which, from my point of view, had been an enjoyable experience with very few problems.

Before moving up to the main line, a mention should be made about the 'Locomotive Exchanges' of 1948. Much has been written about these event, but I would like to place on record the locomotives involved that I was fortunate enough to see in action on the GN line. These were LNER 'A4' 4-6-2 No 60034 *Lord Faringdon* (formerly *Peregrine*); LMS '7P' 4-6-2 No 46236 *City of Bradford*; LMS '6P' 4-6-0 No 46162 *Queen's Westminster Rifleman*; SR 'Merchant Navy' 4-6-2 No 35017 *Belgian Marine*; GWR 'King' 4-6-0 No 6018 *King Henry VI*; and GWR '3800' Class 2-8-0 No 3803. In addition to these locos I also observed Class 'B1' No 61251 *Oliver Bury* depart from St Pancras during the trials. This proved to be a very interesting period in railway history, seeing these 'foreign' locos running over GN metals. All I can say is that it gave me a great deal of pleasure to be able to witness part of the events, and something that I will never forget. As I always carried my camera with me while at work, I was able to take some photographs from the cab of the loco I happened to be working on at the time.

Above Ex-LMS 'Pacific' No 46236 *City of Bradford* leaves King's Cross during the Exchanges.

Below Ex-SR 'Merchant Navy' 'Pacific' No 35017 *Belgian Marine* passes Belle Isle with a dynamometer car during the 1948 Locomotive Exchanges.

Above Ex-GWR 2-8-0 No 3803 with dynamometer car is seen at **Ferme Park.** *Alec G. Ramsdale*

Below Ex-GWR 'King' Class 4-6-0 No 6018 *King Henry VI* passes Hornsey. *Alec G. Ramsdale*

3
THROUGH THE LINKS AT TOP SHED

This chapter will cover the 'main line' part of my firing career, working my way through the four links up to the Top Link, where many of the workings were the well-known named trains, and which will be covered in more detail later. As I have previously explained, all moves were done on a seniority basis. If, for example, there was a vacant diagram to cover in a higher link, which could be a 'Grantham Return', this would be 5 hours' extra pay, so the most senior available fireman from No 4 Link would be booked to work this diagram, then a fireman with less seniority would cover the work with the lower mileage, such as a Cambridge. These situations arose during holidays and sick leave. It sounds a complicated system, but appeared to work very well without any problems

In general there was an assortment of work in No 4 Link, both passenger and freight. The latter was mainly to Hitchin and Peterborough, from the slowest loose-coupled train to the fastest fully fitted freight (fitted with a vacuum brake the full length of the train). Then there were the passenger workings to both Cambridge and Peterborough, which sometimes would be a semi- fast or one of the famous 'Cambridge Buffet' trains, with limited stops. Then there were the slower trains over the Cambridge branch; some terminated at Royston and some at Meldreth, where the loco ran round the stock and worked it back tender-first as a passenger train to Hitchin, where it would be uncoupled and taken to the depot for turning

and topping up the tender with water. At this period the loco would be a Class 'B1' 4-6-0, designed by Edward Thompson. Here we could think about our own meal break, while the train from which we had been uncoupled would be worked to King's Cross by another loco and crew.

On my first day in No 4 link I signed on at 4.35am and worked the 6.05am semi-fast train to Cambridge. I would be firing to a different driver this week as my rostered mate, Sid, was still 'learning the road'. Our allocated loco was No 60108 *Gay Crusader*, which had not yet been converted to left-hand drive so was classified 'A10'; if my memory is correct these locos were re-classified as 'A3' after conversion from right-hand drive, and included some other modifications.

After collecting our issue kit of tools, we walked round to the running shed where work was started on the preparation of the loco. After working on No 69499 for so long it felt strange to be on a 'Pacific', but no doubt I would soon get used to it. Having done all the checks that I would have done on an 'N2', and having spread the fire all over the firebars, boiler pressure began to rise, and both injectors and steam sanders were tested. I then did a general clean-up in the cab, while my driver completed the oiling, then the loco was moved outside the shed to fill the tender with water and trim the coal to make it safe. While all this was going on I started on the fire by filling up the back corners and under the door, leaving the front section of the grate empty;

While the tender is topped up with water, Driver Sid Piggins poses with 'B1' 4-6-0 No 6100 at Royston in 1950. The loco has run round the stock ready to return to Hitchin tender-first.

with the damper closed this would keep the steam pressure down, as we did not want the loco blowing off steam as went down to 'the Cross' tender first through Gasworks Tunnel. Also, the boiler water would be kept at a low level – if boiler pressure started to get too high, the injector could be put on to reduce it by introducing cold water to the boiler.

We backed on to the train standing in Platform 11, where the shunter was waiting to couple us on, and set the head-code, at the same time removing the head-lamp on the tender. By this time the braking system had been tested, and we were ready to leave. I should also add that before we left Top Shed with our loco we had washed and made a can of tea. I would also like to mention that on the ex-GN section it was not part of the fireman's job to couple and uncouple the loco to and from the train; we had to do it when working in the ex-NE section, and when working to Cambridge, which was in the ex-GE section. I do not know the real reason for this situation, but imagine that it was something left over from the pre-Grouping days.

You will probably be surprised that a Gresley 'Pacific' was booked on a Cambridge working, but this particular diagram often had a 'Pacific' on it; it may have had a defect that had now been repaired, and was being 'run in' before going on to express work. Indeed, this diagram was known as the 'running-in turn', and many famous locomotives worked the train over the years.

Having received the 'right away', and all signals being green, my driver opened the regulator and we were off. In the meantime I opened the damper, pushed some of the fire from under the door, spread it over the firebars with a 'bent dart', and entering Gasworks Tunnel with half a boiler of water and a full head of steam. (The purpose of the 'bent dart' was to remove clinker from the back corners and under the door when the fire was being cleaned, but it was also useful for pushing the fire down at the beginning of a trip. The other fire-irons were the 'pricker', used for breaking up the clinker, and the 'clinker shovel', for throwing the clinker out of the firebox when cleaning the fire; they would also be used when dropping the fire in an emergency due to injector failure.)

Above In 1949 I fired on No 60108 *Gay Crusader* on the 6.05am semi-fast train to Cambridge; The loco had not yet been converted to left-hand drive so was classified 'A10'. I am in the cab as we prepare to leave Cambridge.

Right Another 'A10', No 112 *St Simon*, passes the Low Yard and Ferme Park with a down express in 1948.

It was a comfortable trip and we did not encounter any problems, the loco being worked lightly as we only had eight coaches on (it would have been a different story with 12-15 coaches). Passing over the water troughs at Langley I dipped the scoop in to top up the tender, and we continued on to Cambridge, running into one of the bay platforms, where, as stated above, it was my job to uncouple our loco. We were now relieved by a Cambridge crew and made our way to the depot, where we had our meal break and a chat to some of the other crews who would also be taking their break. This made the occasion enjoyable as we were able to socialise with crews from various depots

'B1' No 61090 takes water on Langley troughs in 1950. This is the site of the present-day Stevenage station.

who worked on the ex-GE section, namely Stratford, March and Kings Lynn.

The return trip on this working was to relieve a Cambridge crew on one of the 'Buffet Trains'. On this occasion it was Class 'B17' 4-6-0 No 61663 *Everton*, my first trip on this class of loco, and after the comfort of the 'A10' I was not very impressed with the ride on the 'Footballer': the seats were uncomfortable, and the loco was so rough-riding it was more favourable to stand up. The only thing in the loco's favour was that she was very free-steaming. I must say that it was a pleasure when we ran into 'the Cross' and stopped – it was then possible to sit on the seat without being bounced off.

Having stated my first impressions of the 'B17s', no doubt one got used to the rough ride, as I am sure the GE crews did, as they worked some of the crack trains out of Liverpool Street to many places all over East Anglia. On reflection, any loco without a 'pony truck' (two-wheel bogie) under the cab is going to be a bit rougher, but I do feel that the 'B17s' were the roughest ride I experienced throughout my firing career, and over the years I would be firing on many more of this class of loco. Clearly we 'Northern' men were spoiled with our 'Pacifics' and 'Green Arrow' 'V2s'.

To finish the day we took *Everton* into King's Cross Passenger Loco, where it would be turned and serviced for a Cambridge crew to work it back. So ended my first day in the 'Odd Main Line' link.

It was not very long before my rostered driver, Sid Piggins, 'signed the road', and at first it seemed strange to be firing to him on a main-line loco rather that No 69499, but we soon adjusted to the different class of work. We found ourselves working an assortment of different types of train, mainly with Class 'V2' 2-6-2s, 'B1' 4-6-0s, 'L1' 2-6-4Ts, 'K3' 2-6-0s and 'WD' 2-8-0s, and in addition we would sometimes work on 'A1', 'A2', 'A3', 'A4' and 'A10' 4-6-2s, and also the 'W1' 4-6-4, so in all we had an interesting time.

One day, when working the 6.05am to Cambridge with Sid and an 'A4' that had been in the shops for repairs, imagine my surprise to be told, 'You should know the road to Cambridge by now, so today you take her down, and I'll bring her back.' (When working this diagram earlier it had been modified, hence the reason why we worked the 'B17' on the 'Buffet Express' – this time we would be working the return trip back to 'the Cross' with our own loco on a semi-fast.

Can you imagine how I felt sitting in the driving seat leaving Top Shed, taking the 'A4' down to 'the Cross' and coupling on to the train, knowing that I would be driving to Cambridge? It was a great feeling when Sid called out 'Right away! and I opened the regulator and off we went. Everything was fine and there were no hitches until we were on the Cambridge branch. On running into the station at Ashwell & Morden I under-estimated how fast we were going and overshot the platform by the length of four coaches. After getting authorisation we reversed back into the platform to let the passengers get off. Sid came over to me and said, 'You now know where the platform is, so I very much doubt if you will run through again.' He was right, because in my career both when driving as a fireman under the supervision of the driver, then as a driver in my own right, I never did overshoot that station again, so by doing that I had obviously learned something. Sid always said that the only way to learn the road was by doing the driving, and he was correct.

The platform at Ashwell was at this period very short, holding only a small number of coaches, and driving a 'Pacific' loco is totally different from driving a 'B1' or an 'L1'. 'Pacifics' were built for speed and a smooth ride, so it was easy to underestimate their speed. Very few locos were fitted with speedometers, so it was left to the experienced driver to work out his speed; a few locos were fitted with 'Flaman Speed Recorders', but the number was very limited.

When we arrived in the bay platform at Cambridge, the station pilot, a Class 'C12' 4-4-2T, was waiting to couple on the other end of our train to release us from the platform so that we could then go 'light engine' to the depot, where we went under the coal hopper to fill up the hole in the tender, then on to the turntable to turn the loco. Moving back to the water crane, we topped up the tank, and then it was our turn for a meal break.

I would say we often experienced problems turning 'Pacifics' on the Cambridge table. Our locos were a very tight fit, and it was a problem to get the table correctly balanced; very often we would get halfway round and the table would stick, so the call would go out to the messroom – 'All hands to the table, the Northern men are stuck!' – and before many minutes had passed the messroom would empty and all available drivers and firemen would arrive to assist us, muttering 'Blooming Northern men!' After a great deal of pushing the table would begin to move and the loco would be turned. Turning a loco by hand without the assistance of an electric or vacuum motor was hard work; also, as already mentioned, moving a loco a few inches with the table halfway round to try and rebalance it could be fatal if the loco was only equipped with a vacuum brake; this was slower acting than a steam brake, and the loco could run off the table.

Our Hitchin and Cambridge branch workings were mainly done with Class 'B1' and 'L1' 2-6-4T locos, and we had two unpleasant experiences in one week while working on an 'L1'. The first was on an evening rush-hour train from 'the Cross' to Royston. Most of these trains ran semi-fast, and running bunker-first between Brookmans Park and Hatfield, near Redhall signal box, a union link (part of the Walschaerts valve gear) became uncoupled from the crosshead arm. With lots of banging going on Sid started to brake, slowing down but leaving enough momentum to run slowly into Hatfield station, where a loco came out of the depot to take our 'L1' off to a siding. Then from the depot came our replacement loco, an 'N7'; the crew did not want to leave their regular engine in our care as they had just cleaned and polished everything in the cab, and I must say they had done a great job. We left Hatfield after some 20 or more minutes' delay and worked the train to Royston. After running round we then worked the stock empty to the sidings at Hitchin, and on arrival at the depot there was a Hatfield crew waiting to take their precious 'N7' home. As

for us, we finished our day's work with a Hitchin-based 'L1'.

Some two days later we were working the same train from 'the Cross' with an 'L1', the only difference being that we were smokebox-first, when the unbelievable happened near Redhall box – once again there was crashing and banging from the valve gear, this time on Sid's side, and he shouted, 'Keep your head in – don't look out!'

We eventually limped once again into Hatfield, where on inspection we found that the combination lever had parted company from the union link. Our replacement loco was a Class 'N2' without condensers – on this occasion when we arrived back at Hitchin there was no Hatfield crew waiting for it…

The station staff at Hatfield suggested to us that perhaps it might be a good idea if we stayed at home for the remainder of the week, as we had caused so much dislocation involving two locos being taken out of service, but I am pleased to say that the remainder of the week passed without incident.

Very often on a Sunday we would be booked on an additional turn, and on one occasion I was with Driver Alf Guymer working a special train to Skegness. When signing on duty at 5.30am, Alf was given a sheet with all of our workings for the day. After we had prepared our 'B1', No 61203 (which was in spotless condition), we went 'light engine' to Waterworks Sidings where we backed on to our train of nine coaches. Our special was a charter train, so we now ran as empty stock to Biggleswade, where our first party of passengers were waiting, then on to Sandy to pick up the remainder. There was a short delay here while many crates of beer were loaded into the guard's brake, then we were off to the East Coast.

I should explain that Skegness was not a normal destination for Top Shed drivers, so no drivers at 'the Cross' were 'taught the road' between Peterborough and Skegness. This meant that we would be stopping at Peterborough to top up the tank and pick up our Pilotman, who would be doing the driving to Skegness (he would be based at New England depot).

This working was classed as a 'short lodge

diagram'. On our arrival at Skegness we would be relieved by a Boston depot crew, and we would book off duty and spend the rest of the day at the resort. After spending a day of leisure in glorious sunshine it was time to book on duty as we now had to work our special back home. To me it was like doing two days' work in one, and the last thing I now felt like doing was picking up the shovel (bearing in mind that my alarm had called me at 3.45 that morning).

On arrival at the station we could not see our smart 'B1', and in its place on our train was a grubby looking Class 'K3' 2-6-0; it appears that the Boston crew who had taken over from us had, while cleaning the fire, broken some of the firebars (the loco was fitted with rocker-bars), and the 'K3' turned out to be the Boston Pilot, so we knew that it would probably be a rough trip back, as it was usual practice that the loco standing by as the Pilot would be a poor performer.

We left on time and, as expected, the 'K3' bounced along. It was not possible to sit down, and although I did my best the loco was also a bad steamer. Our New England Pilotman said, 'Roll on Peterborough, so I can get off!'

When we arrived Alf decided to 'whistle up' for the Peterborough Pilot. which should have been standing at the station, but when we arrived there was no Class 'V2', which had been the Pilot – it appears that a previous express had failed and had taken it. So we topped up the tank, got a full head of steam and off we went, next stop Sandy. We eventually arrived with low steam pressure and the boiler water level in the bottom nut, and there we stood while building up both steam and water levels, then off we went to our final stop at Biggleswade. From there we were booked to run empty stock to the sidings at New Southgate, where we arrived some 2 hours late, then it was 'light engine' to Top Shed. The fire was in a terrible state, with the clinker level with the bottom of the firebox door – obviously the fire must have been dirty when the loco left Boston depot. We booked off duty at 2.30 on the Monday morning, then we had to get home. What started off well with a 'B1' had finished as a nightmare with a 'K3'!

Just a couple of weeks after this I was on my way to Rome and Naples by rail. This was the first time I had been abroad – it was early 1950 and an unforgettable experience. One thing that does stick in my memory is the sight of the Nord 'Pacifics' at Calais Maritime, and the locos seen at the Gare du Nord. At least I have a photographic record of the trip. Up to this period the only other 'foreign' railway I had travelled on was in Ireland during 1946, and that too was full of interest. I made a point of visiting various engine sheds, including the GNR one at Amiens Street, Dublin, and the locomotive works near Dublin. One of the very noticeable things was the different gauge, being a little wider at 5ft 3in. One class of loco that I was lucky enough to get on the footplate of was a 4-6-0 named Maeve, which was at Cork. The other thing I recall about the trip was the food and chocolate – there was so much of it! In England we still had rationing, so to be let loose where one could buy mostly anything was to me like being in a 'land of milk and honey' after what we had endured during the war. All in all this was also an interesting trip.

Monday 11 February 1952 will always stick in my memory, as it was the day that the body of the late King George VI was brought by train from Wolferton, the nearest station to Sandringham. It was hauled by Class 'B17' No 61617 Ford Castle to King's Lynn, whence BR 'Standard' No 70000 Britannia worked it to King's Cross. The day before, Sid and I were requested to see the Chief Loco Inspector, and we were told that we were to wait in the down bay at Hatfield with a Class 'B1', standing by as a 'pilot' should the loco fail on the funeral train. We were also requested to wear clean overalls. Sid was then given the 'Special Working Timetable' for the complete workings of the funeral train, even to the point at which it should stop at the platform at King's Cross. Should we have to couple on to the front of the 'Britannia', we understood that the loco would be coming from King's Lynn to King's Cross without stopping or picking up water, and this could have created a problem, but I am pleased to say that everything ran smoothly without a hitch.

On the day in question we signed on duty,

prepared our loco – a specially cleaned 'B1' – left the shed and ran 'light engine' to Hitchin. On arrival we went into the loco depot to turn the loco so that it would be facing 'chimney south'. After making a can of tea we ran light to Hatfield, where we were shunted into the bay platform to await the passing of the funeral train. Our instructions were that, after the train had passed, we were to follow it on the slow road to Potters Bar without catching it up; there the slow line converged with the up main line, on which we remained until we reached Finsbury Park, where we were turned back on to the slow road. At Holloway South we were turned off again to the line taking us to 'Goods & Mineral', and we were then turned into the loco yard at Top Shed. It had been an interesting day, knowing that I had been just slightly involved in a moment of British history.

As I went higher in the link, my seniority would eventually occasionally entitle me to higher-grade work, and I now found myself working with another driver for a week. The work was a 'Grantham Return', and this would be my first trip to Grantham on the shovel. My driver was Joe Burgess, who was in the Top Link and had worked on the Western Region with a Class 'A4' during the 1948 Locomotive Exchanges.

Joe had a reputation for being a good engineman, and this was soon to be proved to me as we departed from 'the Cross' with 14 coaches on. Having passed Holloway North our 'A4' began to accelerate with very little noise from the chimney top. We would run non-stop to Grantham, picking up water at both Langley and Werrington troughs. The long climb to Stoke Summit kept me busy on the shovel, maintaining steam pressure and water levels, and soon we were passing Stoke signal box, 345 feet above sea level and 100 miles from the King's Cross. We then entered Stoke Tunnel, 880 yards long, and soon after emerging we approached Great Ponton, where Joe closed the regulator. We coasted down to Grantham, 105½ miles from King's Cross, where the shunter was waiting to uncouple our loco, and we proceeded light engine to the loco yard.

We turned our 'A4' on the 'angle', which

was three lengths of single track in the form of a triangle with two sets of points. This made easy work of turning, far better than the traditional turntable. We then topped up the tank, I took some clinker out of the fire and pulled some of the coal down ready to make up the fire for our return trip. We then made our way to a wooden shed located in the loco yard to make our tea and eat our sandwiches, chatting to other loco crews from Doncaster, York, Newcastle and Nottingham.

Time goes fast when chatting, and it was soon time to rejoin our 'A4' and make up the fire, keeping 'half a glass' of water in the boiler and about 200lb steam pressure. I telephoned the signalman to say that we were ready to leave the depot, the signal 'came off' and we made our way to the south end of Grantham station to wait in a siding for our Scottish express to arrive, which came in hauled by a Peppercorn Class 'A1' with a Grantham crew. The loco was uncoupled and went off to the loco depot, we were put back on and the shunter coupled us up. As we had a corridor tender the buckeye coupling was used, this being normal practice with these tenders. By this time I had removed our tender tail-lamp and placed it on the front of the loco as 'open lights' – one head-lamp over each buffer. Joe had created a brake on the train of '21 inches' (of vacuum) and we were ready to leave.

I now had a full head of steam – 250psi – a good fire on and three-quarters of a boiler of water. We got the 'right away' and as Joe opened the regulator I spread the fire over the firebox from under the door with the 'bent dart', leaving the back corners built up. We were now beginning the climb up to Stoke, and I was once again back on the shovel. Having cleared Stoke Summit we began the descent to Peterborough, passing through Corby Glen, Little Bytham, Essendine and Tallington, this being the 'racing ground' of the GN line. I had been looking forward to this part of the run, having heard so much about it, and I was not disappointed. Our 'A4' rode like a Rolls-Royce at 90mph, and I was able to sit down and enjoy it, thinking to myself that at last one of my ambitions has been achieved. I recorded that it was a glorious summer day, and the 'A4' was double-blastpipe No 60034 *Lord Faringdon* – these 'A4s' were free steaming.

Having 'dipped' at Werrington troughs, I now started to build up the 'back corners' ready for the climb up to Yaxley. We passed through Peterborough station at 15mph, crossed the bridge over the River Nene and began the climb, passing brickworks on both sides of the railway, which extended from Fletton up to Yaxley; there were dozens of tall chimneys, and the brickworks even had its own steam-worked narrow gauge railway system.

We now crossed Stilton Fen and continued our run towards 'the Cross'. It is a rising gradient from about Tempsford to Stevenage – nearly 20 miles – so I was kept busy on the shovel. Having worked 180 miles without taking on any coal, by this time it was getting further back in the tender, making it harder work. Passing over Langley troughs I lowered the scoop to pick up water, and it was not long before we were crossing Welwyn Viaduct and approaching Hatfield.

We now began our final climb and I was back on the shovel, getting the fire right to see us over Potters Bar, after which it is mainly a falling gradient into 'the Cross' except for a slight rise between Hornsey and Harringay. Joe shut the regulator in the region of Hadley Wood, and we would then coast right into King's Cross, provided that there were no signal checks or speed restrictions. The aim was to run into the terminus with a very low fire, just over 200psi of steam and half a boiler of water with the damper closed. This would enable our relief crew to maintain steam pressure without the loco blowing off at the safety valves, as it would probably be 30-40 minutes before the stock went to the sidings, releasing the engine to go light to Top Shed.

So ended my first trip to Grantham with Joe Burgess, a good engineman – a return trip of 210 miles with an 'A4' on a glorious summer's day. I went home feeling that the day had gone well with no problems, and looking forward to working with Joe on that diagram for the rest of the week.

Then I was once again back with Sid, working our rostered diagrams. On one of the afternoon workings I found that for the first time we would be working double-headed out of 'the Cross' to Hitchin. To my knowledge this was the only diagram where we ran double-headed, and it was on a Peterborough/ Cambridge train. On arrival at Hitchin the leading loco would be uncoupled, moving into a shunt spur, then the train loco would split the train in half, working its portion forward to Cambridge. The other loco would then back on to the other portion to work it forward to Peterborough. This diagram was usually worked by Class 'B1' locos, and before leaving King's Cross the two fireman would agree on who was going to have the first 'dip' at Langley troughs so that they could pick up from half the length of the troughs. I found that we were both able to top up our tanks.

Often people thought that a train was going to leave King's Cross double-headed when they saw two 'Pacifics' emerge from Gasworks Tunnel and appear to be backing on to a train. In fact they would stop short of the train and uncouple, with one loco moving on to its train in another platform, the other backing on to its own stock. This was to save a 'path' from Belle Isle to 'the Cross'; the two locos would have left Top Shed separately, then, under the instructions of the signalman at Belle Isle box, would be coupled together to travel down to the platforms.

A working we often had during April on a Sunday was to Peterborough. This was classed as a 'short lodge' job, and the occasion I am thinking about was a lovely sunny day. We signed on duty and prepared our loco, which on this day was Class 'V2' No 60800 *Green Arrow* – it was her first trip out after coming back from Doncaster 'Plant'. She was spotless and there was a smell of fresh paint. On backing on to our train I noticed that several people were taking photographs – a clean 'V2' was a rare sight and they were making the most of it.

Our train was a special of eight coaches, and we would work it to Peterborough, where the passengers would alight to join a fleet of coaches waiting outside the station to take them on a tour of the Lincolnshire bulb-fields to see the tulips, and also visit Spalding for tea, returning to Peterborough in the late afternoon to rejoin our train back to King's Cross.

A photograph of me in the cab of Class 'V2' No 60800 *Green Arrow* while working a goods train between Stevenage and Hitchin in 1949.

As the months went by I found myself getting nearer to the top of the 'Odd Main Line' link, and would soon be promoted to No 3 Link, this being the 'Main Line Goods'. While working the occasional passenger train, all types of freight trains would be worked, from fully fitted (continuous brakes throughout the train), partially fitted (brakes on only part of the train), and loose-coupled (using only the loco's brake).

After a few more weeks firing to Sid, I found myself rostered in the No 3 Link with Driver Frank Wilson, who would be my driver for the next few months. Of course I was sorry to lose Sid, with whom I had worked for such a long period; from his knowledge I had learned so much that would be invaluable to me throughout my future footplate career. After my move up the No 3 Link I never worked with him again.

In my opinion the 'Main Line Goods' link was not the best of links. This was what I would call the unsocial period of my career –

much of the work was at night, and I found myself at work when all of my friends were going out enjoying themselves. I would be signing on duty in the late afternoon, then booking off in the early hours of the morning, faced with the problem of getting home, or signing on at night and going home when the majority of people were thinking of starting their journey to work. It was at this time that I decided to buy a motorcycle, which did make life easier, and over the years my 'Velocette' gave me great service.

One of the passenger workings in the link was the 'Night Mail', departing from 'the Cross', if my memory is correct, at 10.40pm; this was another 'Grantham Return' diagram. The stock at the front of the train consisted of GPO mail-vans equipped with nets for picking up and dropping mail at speed; on this train it was done at Hitchin South and Huntingdon North, and it was interesting to glance back after the loco had passed the pick-up apparatus to watch the pick-up and drop of the mail. There was very little clearance between the side of the train and the pick-up equipment so, from the footplate crew's point of view, when approaching these points it was a case of 'keep your head in for safety' – which is why I said '*after* the loco had passed the pick-up apparatus'.

On one occasion when working this diagram, while preparing our loco, an 'A3', I had problems getting both injectors to work (the injectors transfer water from the tender to the boiler). Frank had a go and gave up, so we sent for the fitters, who, after some considerable time, managed to get them working. Leaving the shed a few minutes late, we backed on to our train in No 10 platform and, at the booked time, left 'the Cross' with 12 coaches on.

Climbing the bank to Holloway North I was struggling to get the right-hand injector to work, but with no success. I then managed to get the left-hand injector on, but by this time we were between Finsbury Park and Harringay with the water level getting low. I was on the shovel maintaining the steam pressure, then, as we approached New Southgate, the left-hand injector failed. We stopped under the protection of signals at Cemetery signal box, and while Frank informed the signalman of the situation, requesting a replacement loco, I was throwing the fire out to protect the boiler – this was the only occasion throughout the whole of my firing career when I had to drop a fire in an emergency, and it is not something to be recommended.

After blocking the main line for 1½ hours, we eventually left with our replacement loco, 'A2' No 60513 *Dante*, which I believe at the time was based at New England depot. Being a one-off night, I have no note of the name of the 'A3' that failed, but the name of the 'A2' has always been one of my permanent memories, as a great deal happened that night.

After a lot of hard work – starting from scratch to build up the fire – I eventually won the battle with *Dante* regarding both boiler water level, and steam pressure. On our arrival at Grantham we were uncoupled from the train and went 'light engine' to the loco depot, turning, filling the tank and checking the loco ready for our return trip.

While having our meal break we were informed that our return working had been cancelled (it should have been a fully fitted freight), and we were to go 'light engine' to New England depot, leave the loco there, and travel back to King's Cross from Peterborough North; this would include the 45-minute walk from the depot to the station to catch a train. It was a very undesirable finish to a rough night's work – there was only one thing in its favour, that the weather was fine and not pouring with rain.

I now found myself working the fully fitted fish trains from Peterborough to East Goods Yard, where the locos, still manned by Hornsey depot crews, were waiting to work the fish forward to Clapham Junction. I thought back a few years, when I was watching the fish trains arriving from Scotland and Grimsby then working them forward to South London, and it gave me some satisfaction to think that after a short time, a change of depot and working my way up through the links at Top Shed, I was now working some of those very fish trains into East Goods Yard from the north – another of my many ambitions achieved.

On another occasion I was working a No 2-speed freight from King's Cross to Peterborough (half 'fitted' and half loose-coupled) on one of those nights with light rain, best described as a black night with no stars or moon, and heavy cloud. We were turned to the slow line at Hitchin, and on the approach to Three Counties the signalman was waving a green light slowly from side to side to warn us that we had 'broken loose' (one of our couplings had broken, and our train was in two parts). The danger with this was that if we stopped quickly the rear portion of the train might run into the portion to which we were still attached, depending on the gradient of this section of track. We eventually stopped, and to cut a long story short – there were lots of Rules & Regulations to be dealt with – we were able to re-couple our train. One of the coupling links had broken, so we simply used the coupling on the other wagon. A great deal of credit was due to our guard, who dealt with the problem so efficiently, thus reducing lots of delays.

It would have been a different story if the wagon drawbar or coupling hook had broken, creating lots of problems for re-coupling; also, had a coupling broken on the section of our train that was fully fitted, the vacuum pipe would have broken and the brake would have been fully applied automatically; as already pointed out, stopping more quickly increases the risk of a collision, as the rear section might run into the portion that has stopped. The only way the breakaway portion could be stopped was by the guard using the hand-brake in his guard's van. This was not a very good experience, but fortunately it was the only time I worked a train that broke loose – but it had to be on a pitch-black rainy night!

Top Shed had been allocated some additional main-line diagrams, which would occasion further promotion through the links, so I felt that it would only be a few months before I moved up to No 2 Link, which would mainly be main-line passenger work. No 2 Link was a non-lodge link, and any driver or fireman could stay in it, if they did not want to move up to No 1 Link, as that was a volunteer lodge link. So a driver in No 2 could stay there until he retired, and a fireman could stay there until he was eligible to become a 'Passed Fireman' (driver). People had their own personal reasons for not wanting to do lodge work, and were quite happy to stay in No 2 link. For myself, it had always been my ambition to finish my firing career in the Top Link, No 1, the lodge link.

Indeed, after a few months I was again on the move, up to No 2 Link. This would mean that I would no longer be firing to Frank on mainly freight trains, and would also not have to contend with the terrible unsocial hours, which I did not enjoy.

My driver in No 2 Link was Bill Andrews, with whom I got on well. Our first trip together was to Doncaster; this was new to me, as I had never worked north of Grantham. Bill gave me lots of helpful advice about the road, as there were two additional water troughs to replenish the tender, at Muskham, just north of Newark, and Scrooby, just north of Ranskill. On arrival at Doncaster we were relieved by a Doncaster crew who worked the train forward, while we had our meal break in the train crews' messroom on the station.

We then relieved a Doncaster crew and worked a train back to King's Cross, so once again two new sets of water troughs had to be located before we reached Grantham. However, I need not have worried as Bill gave me plenty of warning. One thing I will always remember about my first trip to Doncaster was that the loco going down was a Peppercorn 'A1', while that on the up trip was a Class 'A2/2', No 60504 *Mons Meg*, a Thompson rebuild dating back to 1944, which spent its working life from this date based at New England.

When we relieved the Doncaster crew I noticed that the coal was well back in the tender, so with 156 miles to go I would be kept busy with 13 coaches behind us. We got the 'right away', Bill opened the regulator, I picked up the shovel, and off we went. As predicted, it was hard work right from the start due to the coal being so far back in the tender; instead of sitting on my seat I was in the tender with a coal hammer pulling down the next supply of coal. The best way to describe these locos was 'coal scoffers' – the fireman's seat was always in good condition, simply because there was very little chance of sitting on it. Also, for 'Pacifics' these locos were in my opinion rough-riding, and I am glad that there were only six of them, being rebuilds from the LNER Class 'P2'. I must say that having nearly cleaned out the tender, and having lost I don't know how much sweat, it was good to see Potters Bar, from where it is basically a downhill run to 'the Cross'. So ended my first round trip to Doncaster, and having been on the shovel for 312 miles, I must say I went home tired, and had no problems with sleeping that night – but of course the next day would be a further 312 miles!.

After a few weeks I was soon into the swing of the jobs, and it was satisfying going to work knowing that almost every day I would be working main-line passenger trains.

At about this time I went to Norway for a holiday, and during the journey from Oslo to Andalsnes I had the experience of riding on the footplate from Hamar to Lillehammer. The line hugged the edge of Lake Mjosa, the

Bill Andrews, my driver in No 2
Link.

largest lake in Norway, and the distance travelled on the footplate was 58 kilometres (37 miles). The loco was a four-cylinder compound 4-6-0, and I was able to converse with the fireman who spoke perfect English; however, the driver spoke no English, and it was a great pity that my Norwegian was so limited. It was a wonderful experience, one that I will never forget.

On my return it was back to work with Bill. He was a good engineman and we worked together very well – it was a pleasure to go to work.

Over the past few years I had continued to attend the Mutual Improvement Classes, and as I got nearer to becoming a driver so they became more important to me for the knowledge they provided. Very often a group of us would meet in one of our houses and discuss various aspects of the locomotive or Rules & Regulations – we all agreed that these meetings were an advantage. I would like to add that neither the LNER nor BR in the steam era gave train crews any tuition – everything was self-taught in our own time, the only thing provided being the facilities. The LNER did have a 'Steam Instruction Van', which toured all of the MPDs; this had a collection of cut-away engine parts and was very helpful, but only visited a depot about once a year – and we also had to visit it in our own time. It still functioned in the same way

Above and left Memories of my footplate trip on Norwegian Railway four-cylinder compound 4-6-0 No 354 in 1951.

under the Eastern Region of BR. Many of the models and cut-away engine parts are now in the National Railway Museum at York. We all had a great deal to thank many of the drivers for, who gave up some of their spare time to pass on their knowledge to us.

One day when I signed on duty there was a letter for me, informing me that I would soon be eligible to be moved up to No 1 Link, as there were going to be some vacancies due to the senior firemen being passed for drivers, and would I sign the enclosed paper agreeing to lodge at York, Leeds, Newcastle and Edinburgh? This I did, and within a few weeks I found myself in No 1 Link, the Top Link, with a new driver – Bob Marrable – who was ex-Great Central, having previously worked at Neasden and Woodford, although he had been at King's Cross for the majority of his footplate career.

4
TOP LINK AND 'THE ELIZABETHAN'

I was a fireman in the Top Link for nearly three years, and would now work on a regular engine, this being Class 'A4' No 60017 *Silver Fox*. As was the practice in the 'Met' link there were two sets of men per engine (two drivers and two fireman), who always worked opposite shifts. By sheer coincidence my opposite fireman was a school friend of mine, Sid Webb, with whom I have remained

friends for many years; I had the privilege of being his best man when he took the plunge into marriage. He later became a driver and spent many years at King's Cross, eventually transferring to Southend-on-Sea, from where, after many more years, he retired. Sid's driver's name on *Silver Fox* was George Graham, for whom I never fired.

My first shift on No 60017 was quite a thrill

'A4' No 60017 *Silver Fox* at Peterborough North in 1955.

Two years earlier Driver Bob Marrable is seen in the driving seat of *Silver Fox.*

Myself (left), Bob Marrable and Top Shed shedmaster Mr J. Simpson with *Silver Fox.*

for me. As I climbed up on to the footplate I thought to myself that not many firemen had an 'A4' for their regular engine. The loco was in a lovely condition – the cleaning gang under Dick Ball had done a great job, as they always did with every loco they cleaned.

My first trip with '17', firing to Bob Marrable, was a 'Grantham Return' trip. I found that Bob was another good engineman, and a pleasure to work with. At that time the loco still had a single blastpipe, was light on coal, steamed well, and rode like a Rolls-Royce. We had a very comfortable round trip with no problems. In fact, firemen had a saying about good-steaming locos: show it the shovel and the needle (steam pressure gauge) will not go back. '17' was one of those locos.

The accompanying table gives a summary of the named trains on which I fired during my period at Top Shed, many of them while in

No 1 Link. Unfortunately, although over the years I made many notes, I have no actual recorded dates when I worked on these trains, except that it was between 1950 and 1956, while working through all four of the main-line links.

Although our regular engine was '17', if for some reason she could not be booked out to us we were usually allocated another 'A4', No 60034 *Lord Faringdon.* This loco was fitted with a double blastpipe and was very free steaming, but in my opinion she tended to burn more coal; however, even with inferior fuel the loco steamed well, which did tend to make life easier. There were some diagrams when we would not be allotted our regular engine, and in those instances we would be have an 'A1', 'A2', 'A3', 'A4', 'V2', 'W1' or 'B1', so as you can see we had plenty of variety.

The first lodge turn I was to work would be

Train	Our destination	Train destination
'Aberdonian'	Grantham	Aberdeen
'Elizabethan'	Edinburgh	Edinburgh
	(crew change at Tollerton)	
'Flying Scotsman'	Grantham	Edinburgh
'Heart of Midlothian'	Grantham	Edinburgh
'Norseman'	York	Tyne Commission Quay, Newcastle
'Northumbrian'	Grantham	Newcastle
'Scarborough Flyer'	Grantham	Scarborough
'Tees-Tyne Pullman'	Newcastle	Newcastle
'White Rose'	Doncaster	Leeds and Bradford
'Yorkshire Pullman'	Leeds	Leeds and Bradford

to Newcastle on the 'Tees-Tyne Pullman'. This left Kings Cross at 4.45pm and made its first stop at Darlington, a distance of 232 miles (at a later date an additional stop was made at York), then on to Newcastle, a total distance of 268 miles. On arrival we were relieved by a crew from Gateshead depot, then went off to have a wash and a clean-up before going to a nearby canteen for a much-needed snack. We then made our way to Westmorland Road, where we stay the night in a guest house.

On my first Newcastle trip I was lucky to have a mate like Bob Marrable, who, being a good engineman, made my job a lot easier. As it was springtime the whole run was made in daylight with fine weather conditions, and of course we had our regular engine, No 60017, which was in prime condition. There was an additional water trough at Wiske Moor (making a total of five pick-ups); located about 2 miles north of Northallerton, here we would pick up some 2,000 gallons of water. I found the trip full of interest, going through places that hitherto had only been names to me, like Selby Swing Bridge, Naburn Swing Bridge, York, Darlington and Durham, with its magnificent views of the Cathedral, then over the viaduct at Chester le Street, crossing the River Tyne by the King Edward Bridge and entering Newcastle Central – I now had a visual picture of these places. One very pleasant surprise I had after passing through York was when our guard came through the corridor tender with a welcome can of fresh tea – these corridor tenders did have other uses besides being used for changing the train

crews on the non-stop. I must add that I slept very well that night.

Not all my future trips were as smooth as that one, and there was the odd occasion when things did go wrong: bad coal, poor steaming, a hot bearing, or poor weather conditions – fog, snow, rain – giving slippery rails. In certain conditions the smoke would come down, making visibility a nightmare, especially bearing in mind that many signals were still lit by oil. Many people often consider a steam engine driver's job as being very glamorous, but in reality it was far from it.

The next morning we made our way to Gateshead depot by walking across King Edward Bridge from Newcastle Central for the first time. This was quite an experience, with impressive views down the River Tyne towards the other bridges. A form of catwalk was provided for this purpose, or sometimes we would be lucky enough to hitch a lift on a light engine going from Central station to the depot; very often this was a Class 'V3' 2-6-2T, and was the only time I was ever able to get on the footplate of that class.

On arrival at the depot we would sign on duty and proceed to prepare No 60017, usually assisted by a Gateshead shed crew. Having built up the fire, we would top up the tender with coal, then proceed 'light engine' to Central station to pick up the eight coaches forming the up 'Tees-Tyne Pullman', which left at 9.25am.

Let me explain the coupling procedure. We were now working on the North Eastern Region, where the fireman was responsible for setting up the tender's buck-eye coupling, but the Carriage & Wagon department was responsible for the train coupling, this being supervised by a shunter. Having coupled on, the fireman was responsible for connecting both the vacuum and heater pipes; on the Eastern Region the shunter always did all of those jobs. On the ex-GN section of the Eastern Region it was never the fireman's job to couple on to a train, except when coupling to another light engine, while on the ex-GER section, as already explained, it was the fireman's job.

Our return trip was uneventful, '17' performing very well, and we ran into 'the Cross' just a couple of minutes early. We were relieved on arrival by a Top Shed crew, and were then off duty for just over 24 hours before signing on the next day for the next trip to Newcastle; this was one of the advantages of some of the lodging turns, providing more free time to spend at home.

At one period we worked the 'Flying Scotsman' (10am from King's Cross) down to Newcastle, and lodged there until the following morning, giving us most of the afternoon and the evening off. I recall on one afternoon catching a train to Haltwhistle and doing a great deal of walking to explore part of Hadrian's Wall – which just goes to show how fit I must have been to do this after 268 miles on the shovel! (Needless to say, my mate Bob did not come with me.) On other occasions we both spent a great deal of time at Whitley Bay enjoying the bracing East Coast air, having travelled down there on the Newcastle electric services, so were able to enjoy some leisure from our work.

There was an arrangement that allowed us to change shifts, and we would normally do this for a full week. One week I had a request from Albert Leech to change shifts, to which I readily agreed. At that time he was firing to Driver Bill Hoole on No 60007 *Sir Nigel Gresley*, so that would be my engine for the week and my first time firing to Bill. He was a steam engine enthusiast and took a great deal of interest in the job; in fact, when he retired from BR he moved down to Wales to become a driver on the Ffestiniog Railway. I enjoyed my week working with Bill, although he did tend to work the engine more heavily than my own mate, but we had lots in common as regards railways, and the week simply flew by!

The diagram for which I had changed shifts was a 'Grantham Return', stopping at Peterborough on the down trip. We ran into the 'Excursion Platform', where we were booked to stop for a few minutes while an express passed us on the main line. I began to build up the fire when Bill took the shovel out of my hands and said, 'I always do the firing to Grantham, so my seat is yours for the rest of the trip. You know the road, so she's all yours. Besides, having a go on the shovel helps to keep me fit.'

Bill called out 'Right away', I eased open the regulator and off we went, with me driving No 60007 for my first experience of driving an express from Peterborough to Grantham, which of course included the climb up the bank to Stoke Summit, the highest point of the ex-GNR main line at 345 feet above sea level, and 100 miles from London. As we pulled out of Peterborough on to the main line and passed the New England yards, the loco began to accelerate and I 'wound her up' (reduced the cut-off) then fully opened the regulator while Bill got busy on the shovel. With all clear signals it was not long before Bill was 'dipping the scoop' at Werrington troughs, then at Helpston the climbing began at 1 in 200 through Tallington, Essendine and Little Bytham. By this time I had increased the cut-off, as we went on through Corby Glen at 1 in 178.

The chimney-top exhaust was now a roar as we climbed up to Stoke box, and Bill called across to me to 'drop the lever over' (increase the cut-off even further). This I did, and the exhaust at the chimney top became even more impressive as we passed Stoke box and, sounding the whistle, entered the 880 yards of Stoke Tunnel. On emerging from the tunnel I closed the regulator, having already put on the jet or 'blower', so we could coast down the 1 in 200 through Great Ponton and stop at Grantham, where the shunter was waiting to uncouple our loco, which we took 'light engine' to Grantham depot. That had been my first experience of driving an express train from Peterborough to Grantham, and I enjoyed every minute of it, making me even more determined to pass my driver's examination. But there would be some 18 months to two years before this happened.

That driving routine remained the pattern for the week, which passed very quickly and was a week that I will never forget – and once again I was able to gain some valuable experience, which at some future date I would be able to use.

It is strange how things work out, and although I fired to many of the Top Link drivers during my spell at King's Cross, I never fired to Bill Hoole again. Some of the drivers I did fire to were Joe Howard, Charlie Simmons, Fred Dines, Harry Smith, Bert Cull, Ted Hailstone, Jim Edwards, Percy Heavens, Sid Tapping, Alf Guymer and Alf Smith. There were others, but I regret that I am unable to recall their names, as I did not make a note of every driver with whom I worked. Generally speaking most drivers and firemen worked well together – manning a steam locomotive was a team job, and without it the task would be intolerable. There was the odd isolated case where a driver and fireman did not agree with each other, but this situation was very rare. As you both had the same interest and aim – to get the best possible performance from the locomotive – a great deal of satisfaction was gained from achieving that.

In a couple of weeks we would be working the non-stop from King's Cross to Edinburgh, doing four round trips and working eight days, Sunday to Sunday, and staying at Edinburgh overnight. This would be my first experience of working 'The Elizabethan', another of my ambitions that was soon to become a reality. Sunday quickly came and I signed on duty, complete with a case containing a change of clothes that would be required later. As 'The Elizabethan' did not run on Sundays, we would work a stopping train down to Edinburgh, stay the night, then work the non-stop back on Monday morning. On the Sunday the footplate crew would change over at Tollerton just as they did when working on the non-stop on weekdays.

We walked round to the shed where another crew had already started to prepare our gleaming 'A4' *Silver Fox*. Having

Bert Cull was one of many drivers I fired to while at Top Shed. Here he is seen in the cab of *Silver Fox* with his fireman, Jim Wilson, at King's Cross in 1951.

completed the preparation and made the tea, we were ready to go 'light engine' down to 'the Cross'. There we backed on to our train and met the Haymarket crew who would be relieving us at Tollerton, using the corridor tender. The first compartment in the first coach nearest the loco was reserved for the footplate crew, so this was where our cases went, and where the Haymarket crew would be riding 'on the cushions' prior to relieving us.

All signals were green and off we went. Very often on a Sunday there were delays due to engineering work, as well as long diversions, which made the journey even longer, but today we were lucky – there were a few minor permanent way (PW) restrictions, but no diversions, so we should have a good trip. There were also no big lumps of coal to contend with, as the loco had been coaled at King's Cross Passenger Loco with the best-quality coal, all the large lumps having been broken up; doing it that way also filled the tender to its maximum capacity, which was essential due to the high mileage involved.

Our loco was performing very well and we were running well to time as we emerged from Peascliffe Tunnel and the corridor door opened. The Haymarket fireman handed me a fresh can of welcome tea, and after a quick few words to say that we were having a good trip, he rejoined his driver 'on the cushions'. On the approach to York I began to build up the fire as it would not be very long before we were relieved. Sure enough, just before we reached Tollerton the Scots crew emerged from the corridor and entered the footplate. That would be the end of our work for today, as we left the footplate to go back to our reserved compartment in the train.

This was where the change of clothes was required, as we now had a wash, cleaned up and changed into our 'civvies'. It was then time to have lunch at our reserved table in the dining car, whose staff looked after us very well. Having enjoyed our meal it was time to return to our compartment to enjoy the rest of the scenic ride along the Northumbrian coast – and to think that we were getting paid for doing it!

I was just beginning to settle down to admire the magnificent scenery when Bob reminded me that it would soon be time for me to take a fresh can of tea through to the Scots crew. I therefore made my way to the buffet car, where I was presented with the can of tea and some buns. We were now just north of Alnmouth, and it was my turn to return to the footplate to pass over the tea and buns to our relief crew, which were very much appreciated. I noticed that by this time the coal was beginning to get further back in the tender, which of course made firing a great deal harder work. After a short conversation, I returned to the train. (For these short visits back to the footplate I always had with me a spare overall jacket to keep my 'civvies' clean.)

While sitting in the comfort of our compartment we were often approached by passengers inquiring if it was possible for them to go on to the footplate. This, of course, was against all the Rules & Regulations, and could be dangerous if, say, the visitor was to slip, as the tender plate was moving about all the time with the oscillation of the loco and tender; although the 'A4s' were very smooth riders, we were used to any movement, but a stranger would not! So I am sorry to say that we had to disappoint many people.

By now we were crossing the River Tweed by the Royal Border Bridge, and the view from the train was spectacular. Bob told me that we would soon be passing the England-Scotland border sign, so I had the window open with my camera at the ready. I saw the sign in the distance and managed to take two photographs, which turned out to be successful. We eventually arrived at Edinburgh Waverley and, after having afternoon tea in the restaurant car, Bob led the way down Princes Street to Lothian Road, where Mrs Ronaldson welcomed us to her guest house; this was located opposite the ex-LMS Princes Street Station and the rear looked towards Edinburgh Castle. So here I was at last, staying in Edinburgh having worked a train halfway from London. But tomorrow would be the day, working the second part of the non-stop 393 miles back to King's Cross.

Having had a good night's sleep, Mrs

Above On the run north of Berwick Bob alerted me to the lineside 'Across the Border' sign, so I soon had the carriage window open with my camera at the ready to get a shot.

Below No 60017 *Silver Fox* ready to leave Edinburgh Waverley station with the up 'Elizabethan'.

I emerge onto the footplate from the corridor tender ready to take over firing 'The Elizabethan' south from Tollerton to 'the Cross'.

Ronaldson prepared an excellent Scottish breakfast for us and we made our way by bus to Haymarket loco depot, where we booked on duty and met up with our opposite mates, the Scots crew. After climbing on to the footplate of '17', we rode 'light engine' to Waverley station, where we were coupled on to 'The Elizabethan', booked to depart at 9.45am.

Bob and I made ourselves comfortable in our compartment, and the train left sharp on time to begin the non-stop journey to London, while we enjoyed the passing scenery. In the region of Alnmouth Bob reminded me that it was time to take a can of tea through to the footplate for our mates, which I did with the compliments of the buffet car crew. As we approached Newcastle it was time for the first lunch sitting, so off we went to the dining car, where we were served

an excellent meal. We then made our way back to the compartment and changed into our overalls ready to relieve our mates on the 'front'. Just prior to Tollerton we made our way through the corridor tender to relieve the Scotsmen, who made their way back to the train after saying that the engine was doing well, and that they were having a good trip.

We passed the northbound 'Elizabethan', with blasts on the chime whistle doing it justice, then, passing through York, I was on the shovel in earnest, finding it hard work as the coal was beginning to be further back in the tender. We continued to make good progress, and on the descent of Stoke Bank a welcome Scots voice said that it was time for tea and cake; the fireman handed me a can of tea with a bag of cakes, then made his way back to the luxury of the 'cushions'.

After passing through Peterborough I found myself in the tender pulling the coal forward using the coal hammer and shovel, then it was back to the footplate to feed the fire. This was hard work because the same coal had to be manhandled twice, so, like the train, the shovelling was also non-stop. I must say that the sight of Potters Bar was very welcome, as we would soon be coasting for the last 12-13 miles to 'the Cross'. The coal was now well back in the tender – in fact, it took several paces before I reached it. I quite envied the Midland men with their coal-pushers in the tenders of the 'Duchess' 'Pacifics'.

This was my first trip on 'The Elizabethan' and was very satisfying. We ran into King's Cross at 4.15pm, having done the 393-mile trip non-stop without any snags. I had been one of the two firemen working the longest non-stop run for a steam locomotive in the world. I must say that, when travelling home after being relieved by a Top Shed crew, I was looking forward to the following morning when once again I would be working down to Edinburgh on the non-stop.

The only disadvantage with the non-stop diagram was the fact that, having booked off duty at approximately 5pm, we would book on again at 8am next morning, having 13 hours at home, then it would be off to Edinburgh again, staying there for just under 18 hours before working back to 'the Cross'. Worked out across the four round trips, most of the time off duty was spent in Edinburgh, which was why some Top Shed crews would not do 'lodge work', preferring to have their leisure time at home.

Personally, I enjoyed my long stays at Edinburgh and put the time to good use, visiting all the usual sights. On several occasions I was lucky enough to be there for the Edinburgh Festival, so was able to see some of the events. A few trips were also made to North Berwick, with a boat trip round Bass Rock, then there was the ride across the Forth Bridge to Dunfermline, and a trip on the ferry beside the Forth Bridge, crossing the Firth of Forth from South Queensferry. These were just a few of the trips I was fortunate enough to make, the majority of them with my mate Bob or George Tee, who became my driver when Bob retired. I must say that the highlight of my trips was to walk across the Forth Bridge

with Bob Marrable and Jimmy Swan; Jimmy was the Haymarket driver with whom we were working that week, and it he who got us a pass and permission to walk the full length of the bridge. We were very lucky to have a lovely summer evening to enjoy this unforgettable experience. By now you have probably gathered that I enjoyed my stays in Edinburgh, and you would be correct – I looked upon it as a chance of a lifetime. I was also in Edinburgh for the last week that the tramway system operated before it was replaced by buses, so have a photographic record of the last trams.

About this time I was off to Norway again for my holiday, armed with a footplate pass issued to me by the Norwegian State Railways to ride on the loco from Oslo to Myrdal, where I would be changing to join the train to Flam. This was another great experience, riding on a 4-8-0 four-cylinder compound with a working steam pressure of 228psi, making it a powerful

One fine evening in August 1953 Haymarket driver Jimmy Swan obtained permission for Bob and I to walk the full length of the Forth Bridge, an unforgettable experience.

In 1953 I had a footplate ride on this 4-8-0 locomotive from Honefoss to Myrdal on the Oslo-Bergen line. The engine is seen at Oslo prior to departure.

loco. Finse, the highest point on the line, is 4,299 feet (1,322 metres) above sea level, so there were many mountains to climb! I actually joined the footplate at Honefoss, and to see how this loco was worked on the gradients was something I shall never forget. What made the trip more interesting was that both the driver and fireman spoke very good English, so we were able to converse – and, yes, I did have a go on the shovel, between admiring the magnificent scenery.

On returning to work I found that my first week was a 'Leeds Lodge', which involved working the 'Yorkshire Pullman' down to Leeds, stopping at Doncaster and Wakefield. At Doncaster we were given a jug of tomato juice by the Pullman car staff (Bob told me that in the winter we got a jug of coffee), which was very much appreciated by us. On arrival at Leeds Central we were relieved by a Copley Hill crew, and made our way by bus to Farnley, where fish and chips was purchased in a local shop. We then went to Farnley depot (just a few minutes' walk) and reported to the shed foreman, who had already made arrangements for us to stay overnight in the hostel.

This hostel was very basic – no meals were provided, which was why we took in our own food. We also cooked our own breakfasts with food brought from home. I always had

difficulty sleeping here: because the hostel was sited at the depot it was noisy with loco movements, locos blowing off, and the coaling plant – lying in bed it was possible to hear every lump of coal going into the tender – so as you can imagine sleeping was a problem. A billiard table and dartboard were provided for recreation.

After a restless night's sleep, and having cooked our breakfast, we made our way to Copley Hill depot to book on duty. Having prepared our loco we went 'light engine' to Leeds Central station, where our King's Cross-bound train awaited us. It departed at 9.50am, and it was a steady climb out of Leeds to Ardsley, the latter part of it being 1 in 100. We passed Ardsley loco depot and the extensive yards used for the coal traffic, this part of Yorkshire then being a major coal-mining area, then it was downhill to Wakefield, and Bob would soon be closing the regulator to coast to our first station stop there.

Our next stop was Doncaster, and we arrived on time. As the 'Plant' was at Doncaster it was usual to see something of interest as regards locomotives that had just come out of the Paint Shop, looking immaculate after their overhaul. By now I was back on the shovel as we left Doncaster, and, after losing buckets of sweat, 156 miles later we ran into 'the Cross' and were relieved. It would now be some 26 hours before we would book on duty to work our next trip to Leeds.

There were the odd diagrams that did test one's fitness. One such was the 'Norseman'. After booking on duty we walked down to 'the Cross' and relieved a Top Shed crew who had prepared the loco and taken it 'light' down to the terminus, where they were waiting, already coupled on to the train. This was called 'EPT' ('engine prepared on train'), and we relieved them about 5 minutes before the train was booked to leave. I naturally hoped that the fireman had filled up the back corners, building up a good fire to give me a good start. The 'Norseman' went to Tyne Commission Quay at Newcastle and connected with a Bergen Line ship bound for Norway.

This train was a spare engine diagram, and any loco, from an 'A1' to a 'V2', was used – it would very often be an 'A3'. After a quick few words with the crew that we were relieving, the whistles were blowing and we had the 'right away'; within 10 minutes of stepping on to the footplate we were entering Gasworks Tunnel heading for York. It was not long before I was on the shovel and the injector was on to maintain the boiler water level; it also was not long before I was into the tea-can, as we would be at York before any further tea could be made.

This diagram, a 'York Return', was our heaviest for work content – 376 miles on the shovel for a day's work was 'hard graft'. On arrival in York we were relieved by a North Eastern crew, who worked the train forward to Newcastle. We had between 45 and 50 minutes before we relieved on an up express to work back to London, with a loco that had worked through from Newcastle. By the time we had washed our hands, made the tea and eaten our sandwiches, and made a further can of tea for our trip home, it was time to board our homeward-bound train. As you can imagine, we had very little time at York, and this could be made worse if on the down trip we experienced delays with signals or PW restrictions. So, within a few minutes of eating my snack I would be back on the shovel, this time working harder due to the coal being

further back in the tender. I still marvel that we did not suffer with stomach problems! The homeward trip was often a Gateshead loco, which might not be one of their best, so not only was it a long day's work, but having a poor steamer or a rough-riding loco also did not help.

I can recall on one occasion when working up on this diagram, just past Doncaster the left-hand gauge glass broke, filling the cab with steam and water. I grabbed my jacket and threw it over gauge glass column, pulling down both the steam and water shut-off cocks, which brought some sanity into the cab. I now had the job of fitting a new gauge glass between firing to the loco and keeping a lookout ahead. Unscrewing the nuts on the column was a nightmare, as they had probably not been touched for months; I was also standing on a moving platform near the firebox door, so everything was very hot – just the sort of unwanted incident to round off a 376-mile diagram nicely. I must say that I never had any problems sleeping on that diagram, but what I did suffer was a problem with my hearing. For the whole of the evening I would hear the noise of the loco's valve gear and the general noise associated with a steam engine, and I can only put this down to the high mileage and the number of hours we were actually working on the footplate. By the morning my ears were back to normal. As a point of interest, on this diagram there were eight occasions when water would be picked up from the troughs, four each way.

To the best of my memory the week's work that included the 'York Return' diagram consisted of that trip on Monday and Tuesday, Wednesday off duty, Thursday 'York Return' again, Friday down to Newcastle, and Saturday up from Newcastle. The train worked from Newcastle was 14 coaches, two more vehicles from Scarborough being attached at York, making a grand total of 16 to King's Cross. This was one of the few trains where additional coaches were attached at York, and running into the terminus with such a long train was not a normal working and could create some problems with shunting. To get a shunt loco on to the rear sometimes meant that it would have to go 'light engine' from King's Cross to Belle Isle, cross over from the down to the up tracks, and return to the terminus to allow it to get to the empty stock – fortunately this did not happen very often.

While Bob was still my mate we ran into 'the Cross' one afternoon, and on being relieved Bob was requested to call in to the general office, where representatives of Services Watches presented him with a very nice wristwatch, which also had a stopwatch built into it. The object was to get publicity for the company's products, and it was not long before in the daily press a large advertisement appeared showing a Class 'A4' on the 'Tees-Tyne Pullman' with the caption: 'Driver Bob Marrable drives the Tees-Tyne Pullman train from King's Cross to Newcastle, keeping time with his Services Watch'. This appeared in many daily newspapers for some considerable time.

Then to our surprise we ran into 'the Cross' early one morning (we were on nights) to be met by a Loco Inspector who asked us if we would be prepared to work with the BTC (British Transport Commission) film unit, as they were to make a film all about 'The Elizabethan'. A record was to be made of the longest non-stop journey in the world for a steam locomotive, and it was our diagram the next week. We both thought it was a great idea and agreed to work with the film unit to the best of our ability. The Inspector said that he had been informed that we would be

The indicator board for down 'Elizabethan' at King's Cross, summer 1954.

working with our own engine, *Silver Fox*. I felt quite excited about the prospect of being involved in the making of this film, as I felt that in years to come it would probably become historic. As one of my great interests was still and cine photography, that would make the event doubly interesting from my point of view.

On the following Monday morning we signed on duty as normal for working the non-stop, and were requested to report to the Loco Inspector. Our loco had been prepared for us, and we were to leave the shed early, as some filming was to be done while we were backing on to our train down at 'the Cross'. We made the tea, then walked to the front of the shed where our gleaming '17' was waiting for us. She was spotless on this lovely sunny morning – lucky film crew!

Off we went 'light engine' down to King's Cross, where we are filmed backing on to our train. Various shots were taken, then it was time to go. Bob sounded the whistle, opened the regulator and we are off, with one camera filming from the platform and another near the entrance to Gasworks Tunnel, where we sounded the whistle to its advantage. The crew with whom we would be working for the full duration of the film was Driver Tony Macleod and Fireman Mungo from Haymarket depot. The film was made over a period of roughly two weeks, being filmed at various locations on different days. Some of the footplate shots were filmed separately on other days, and some were filmed when the train arrived at Edinburgh.

We passed through Peterborough North station on the main line, and as we passed the North Box over on the Midland line a Class '3F' ('Jinty'), propelling a parcels van with the doors open inwards and cameras at the ready, began to accelerate, keeping level with us for the whole distance to just north of Helpston, where the Midland line veers off to the left towards Stamford. This meant that filming could be done for a distance of just over 8 miles running parallel with us, and included picking up water at Werrington water troughs. During the course of the week two runs were made at this point of the filming, and credit must go to the cameraman, who, in my

Filming *Elizabethan Express*: (left to right) Firemen Mungo and Ruffell, Chief Inspector Sam Jenkins, and Drivers Marrable and Macleod.

opinion, did a very good job. (I would like to say that the left-side cylinder cock that you can see blowing in the film did not blow all the way from 'the Cross' – it only started as we passed through Peterborough North.)

Much of the filming was done on 'The Elizabethan' itself, showing shots from the train at various locations, with interior sequences showing the passengers, dining car staff, and in the kitchen with the chef.

Filming on the footplate would not have been practical on a service train, as space was very limited, and with a two-man camera crew on board it would have been difficult for the fireman to carry out his duties, so this was done on a special train. Hooks were fitted on each side of the cab roof, which had straps fitted to it to support the camera. When the cameraman was in position there was very little space to work – he had the camera

wedged against his body to reduce movement – and he told me afterwards that his body was black and blue from the buffeting of the camera caused by the oscillation of the loco. When I saw the results of his filming he did a good job under difficult conditions. Most of the filming in the cab was done over a period of two days between King's Cross and Grantham, and 'A4' No 60030 *Golden Fleece* was the loco used; it also appears in some photographs taken afterwards of the footplate crews and the BTC film unit crew.

The Haymarket crew stayed in London for most of the week while this part of the filming was being done. A considerable amount was filmed at Top Shed during the preparation of the loco, and shots were made walking through the corridor tender, together with a shot of the loco leaving the shed.

We had now worked with our Scots

The entire *Elizabethan Express* crew.

colleagues and the camera crew for two weeks, and we all agreed that it had been a great experience. We were promised a preview of all the film taken before it went to the cutting room, and a few weeks later we were invited to the BTC film unit in London to see it. They had made a good job of it, and I was sure a good film would emerge from the material. Unfortunately the finished film eluded me for many years; in fact, I never thought any more about it until one day I decided to write and see if my local management could trace it, and they replied to say that they would do their best on my behalf. Then out of the blue I received a phone call from Mr Harris of Walton Films, who told me that they had taken over the films produced by the BTC film unit, and invited me to visit them at Walton House in London to have a tour of their works, and to see *Elizabethan Express* in their private cinema, when Mr Harris would present me with a copy of the film.

I was surprised that the film only ran for 20 minutes, as so much filming had been done. However, the completed film is very good, providing an historic record of the non-stop journey. I presume that any unused material was discarded in the cutting room when the film was edited, and for what it is worth I feel that much of the unused material would without doubt have produced a more interesting film. Some years later I had the opportunity to speak to transport film historian John Huntley about the missing footage, but to my knowledge he was unable to trace it.

A few weeks later my mate Bob was due to retire as he would be 65; at the time it was the practice at Top Shed to retire on the day of the 65th birthday, and to work the 'Flying Scotsman' down to Grantham, returning with another express. This brought to an end Bob's long railway career, but I would not be working with him on his last day as the job was a fireman's diagram working, and the

I am presented with a copy of *Elizabethan Express* by Mr Harris of Walton Films in the winter of 1973.

driver who should have been working it always volunteered to give it up for the one day, agreeing to work another available diagram. After Bob retired I went to visit him several times at his home near Wembley, but unfortunately early in retirement he became seriously ill, from which he was unable to recover.

From the day that Bob retired my new driver was George Tee, who had started his career at Doncaster, although he had been at King's Cross for many years. A few weeks after we had teamed up we signed on duty to work the 'Tees-Tyne Pullman' and were informed that a VIP and Loco Inspector George Manyard would be riding with us to Newcastle. The VIP was Mr Ronald Nelson, who would be timing us for the entire trip, and part of it is recorded in his book *Locomotive Performance: a footplate survey* (Ian Allan, 1979).

Our loco on this occasion was 'A4' No 60034 *Lord Faringdon*, and after preparing it and running 'light engine' down to King's Cross, we backed on to our train in No 10 platform where Mr Nelson was waiting for us. After coupling on we all stood on the platform to have photographs taken, then it was time for us to depart, the first stop being York (the timings of this train had recently been altered by the additional stop at York). What I remember of the weather is that it was not very good, and due to the time of year darkness descended early in the trip.

No 60034 was fitted with a 'Kylchap' double blastpipe, which made it free-steaming, so we had a good trip down, with George Manyard giving me the occasional break on the shovel – he said that he enjoyed doing some of the firing, and once again I heard the phrase 'It helps to keep me fit'. I am sure that Mr Nelson also enjoyed his trip, making use of his two stopwatches and making lots of notes.

Working some of the crack trains on the railway system, we frequently had VIPs riding on the footplate, always accompanied by a Loco Inspector. There was one big snag with four people on the footplate of a locomotive – there were only two seats, one being occupied by the driver for the whole journey, and the other being used by the guest. When the fireman wanted a short break in his seat the guest usually had the courtesy to vacate it, but unfortunately sometimes there was one who, having sat in the fireman's seat, thought it was his for the trip. However, having put him in the picture that the fireman did enjoy a brief break sitting down, there were usually no further problems, and hopefully the guest still enjoyed the trip, even if he did have to stand for part of it!

One Sunday in summer, when George and I were working back from Edinburgh, engineering work on the track meant that the Scots crew had some diversions, which caused delays, and when we relieved them at

On 4 August 1954 'A4' No 60034 *Lord Faringdon* averaged 73mph between York and Darlington on the *Tees-Tyne Pullman*. Recording the run was Ronald Nelson (with pipe), who is seen with Inspector George Maynard (left), myself and Driver George Tee at King's Cross. *W. J. Reynolds, author's collection*

Tollerton we were well behind schedule. Being a normal service train, the load was heavier than the non-stop, and there were more stops, so by the time we made our way on to the footplate the coal was well back in the tender. We stopped at Doncaster to pick up a Pilotman, who would be piloting us on our diversion to Peterborough via Lincoln and Spalding, as George did not 'know the road'. We were booked to stop at Spalding for water, and while the tank was filling I began to shovel the coal forward in the tender; the Scots fireman whom I had relieved came in the tender with the spare shovel to assist me, and between us we shovelled all of the coal forward from the rear of the tender (coal that had laid there for months) – as you can imagine, I was extremely grateful for his assistance.

We got 'right away' for Peterborough, and our Pilotman passed comment that we would be lucky to get to 'the Cross' with that amount of coal. 'It looks like a lot of rubbish – it's probably been on there since the tender was built.'

On approaching Peterborough the Pilotman suggested that we should whistle up for the pilot as 'fresh engine', but George did not want to give up our 'A4', which on this occasion was No 60009 *Union of South Africa*, which was allocated to Haymarket. So, after stopping at Peterborough and our Pilotman wishing us luck as he left us, George said that if the worst came to the worst we would stop at Hitchin for another engine. We kept going, losing a few more minutes as George nursed her along, and were delighted to go over Potters Bar knowing that it was now downhill to 'the Cross'. Because of the amount of coal that had been used the clinker in the firebox was level with the bottom of the firebox door, and I had by now cleaned out the tender. Passing through Finsbury Park with no fuel, fortunately we had all clear signals into 'the Cross', and I can remember stepping off the footplate on to No 4 Platform exhausted. That was the only time during my firing career that I ran out of coal. We learned afterwards that after the empty stock had gone to the sidings,

Right Myself and Driver George Tee in the cab of 'A4' No 60009 *Union of South Africa.* Alec G. Ramsdale

an 'N2' had to be coupled on to the 'A4' to tow it away to Top Shed. I certainly did not envy the person who had to clean the fire. One thing is for certain – the tender would have a full consignment of fresh coal in it.

One day we arrived at Gateshead depot to sign on duty for the 'Tees-Tyne' up to London, but '17' was missing, and in her place we had a Class 'A1' booked to us. It appears that '17' had been used on an overnight trip to Edinburgh, and had not made it back in time for our working. A Gateshead crew had prepared the loco for us, so all we had to do was make the tea and go 'light engine' to Central station for our train. I do not imagine that Top Shed was very pleased about one of its engines going missing to the Scottish Region – the telephone lines were probably red hot between Top Shed and Gateshead!

Back on 'The Elizabethan' it was not all

Below Union of South Africa at Edinburgh Waverley with 'The Elizabethan' in 1954.

smooth running, and there were times when, due to unforeseen circumstances, we had to stop. I was very fortunate that, over a period of three summers working this train, I can only recall being stopped on two occasions. The first was descending Stoke Bank, when we were stopped by signals at Little Bytham and informed by the signalman that there were cows on the line; after standing there for some considerable time while PW staff cleared the line, our signal was cleared and we continued with all clear signals to 'the Cross'. This of course was very frustrating from everybody's point of view, both passengers and train crew – the train had run non-stop from Edinburgh to Little Bytham, a distance of just over 300 miles, only to be stopped by a herd of cows.

The second time was very tragic. We had passed through Grantham going north, and were running through a cutting, about to enter Peascliffe Tunnel, when George shouted at me with a face as white as a sheet that someone had just run under our wheels. By this time we were in the tunnel and George had fully applied the brake. Our speed at the time of the incident would have been in the region of 80mph, so we stopped at Barkston signal box and I ran to warn the signalman, who immediately put all of his signals back to Danger to stop an up express. After some delay, while we and our guard checked both the loco and the train, we continued on our journey north to be met by officials at Edinburgh. In my opinion George was a hero to be capable of working the train forward to Tollerton, where we were relieved by the Scots crew. We knew nothing about the circumstances that had led to the incident, but we were later informed that the person had not died and survived the injuries, so it did have a happier ending.

The locos at this period were very well maintained and reliable, but once again there was always the occasion when things went wrong. One Saturday we were working up from Newcastle with an 'A4' – I have no record of the loco number – when on the approach to Northallerton we could smell 'pear drops', which indicated that our 'middle big end' was running hot (this was a device fitted to the joint to warn enginemen that

there was a problem). We stopped at Northallerton to examine the loco, confirming that the big end was indeed hot. We informed the signalman that we would require a replacement loco, which would be coming from Darlington, and in the meantime we uncoupled our 'A4' and were able to move it into a siding. Eventually the Darlington pilot, an 'A3', arrived and was coupled up to our train. We continued our trip to London running about an hour late, not the sort of thing that enhances an enginemen's working day, and very undesirable on a 268-mile diagram.

I also recall working a train from Leeds to King's Cross late on a Sunday afternoon during the winter, and we arrived at Wakefield to be told that there was an obstruction blocking the line to Doncaster, and we were to be diverted via York; a Pilotman was provided as George did not 'know the road'. After some delay our signals 'came off', and we continued on our way to York. Neither George nor I had ever been over this road before, so it was all new to us; we passed through stations that we had seen in the working timetables, and I found it interesting to be able to put a place to the name. However, firing over a road without knowing anything about it as regards gradients, etc, is not easy, and by this time it was dark, which made the diversion appear even longer. I do recall going through Harrogate and seeing Starbeck shed, and going over the viaduct at Knaresborough and passing through the station there, then Cattal, Hammerton, Poppleton and on to York, so we were still facing south as we headed for 'the Cross'. We had started from Leeds, 187 miles from London, and here we were at York, still 188 miles from London. I cannot remember how late we were arriving, but it was several hours and I stepped off the footplate exhausted. As the hours got longer, the shovel got heavier and the coal got further back in the tender. It was late by the time I arrived home and, yes, I did sleep well that night.

One afternoon during the summer of 1954 I had the privilege of meeting Canon Eric Treacy, who was busy taking photographs in the area of Goods & Mineral signal box. He was standing at the outlet signal from Top Shed as I was phoning the signalman to tell him that we were working the 5.30pm 'Yorkshire Pullman' from 'the Cross'. While waiting for the signal we invited him into the cab of our 'A4', which that day was No 60034 *Lord Faringdon*. I had already seen many of Eric Treacy's photographs, and knew he was a very good railway photographer, so for me it was a great pleasure to meet him. As our signal cleared, he said that he would be taking a photograph of our train as we climbed up past Belle Isle, and would I oblige with some smoke. After quickly having our photograph taken in the cab, we shook hands with Canon Treacy and he climbed back down to the ground.

He was true to his word, and as we climbed up past Belle Isle he was waiting with his camera. I obliged by producing some effective smoke, and the resulting photograph is very good (see the frontispiece) and appears in books of his photographs. I must add that Eric Treacy sent George Tee and myself some excellent copies of the photograph, which take pride of place in one of my many railway photograph albums.

One other incident that gave us a few bad moments was working down to Leeds on a winter's evening. It was one of those very black nights with heavy cloud and no sign of the moon, and we were running down towards Wakefield when suddenly we cracked some detonators. George made an emergency brake application, and called out that there was a red light being waved about ahead. By this time we had passed the red light and were cracking further detonators. Lots of things went through our minds as we slowed down, and when we came safely to a stop we both breathed a sigh of relief – we had hit nothing and could see nothing ahead.

After a short time a guard climbed into our cab and said that he had carried out full train protection (it had been him waving the red light) as his train had failed, but someone on the failed train had corrected the fault and moved forward to Wakefield without him. I will not go into the finer details of this failure, except that we proceeded with caution to the next signal, where the signalman at Wakefield gave us further instructions.

Some people are luckier than others, and I consider that I was one of the fortunate ones. When I moved into the Top Link I was its junior fireman, and now I was its senior one, which meant that I would have spent the maximum length of time in that link, so it would not be very long before I took my driver's examination, having completed nearly 14 years' service. Accordingly, in early June 1956 I received a letter to the effect that I would be taking my driver's examination within a couple of weeks, and that I would be rostered as a fireman in the 'Yard Link' working on Class 'J52' steam locos and 350hp diesel-electric shunters (late Class 08); the latter, newly built, had just been allocated to Top Shed. It was normal practice to be finished with main-line work, and my last week with George was on the 'Newcastle lodge' working the 'Tees-Tyne Pullman', so I finished my main-line firing in style, feeling a little sad as I ran into King's Cross as a fireman for the last time.

It seemed strange after working so hard over so long a period to be back working on shunting duties. After a few days I was booked to see a Loco Inspector to learn how to make all the various 'trimmings' used for loco lubrication purposes. We then walked down to King's Cross station and boarded the footplate of a Class 'N2', which I drove 'all stations' to Hertford North under the watchful eye of the Inspector. We then travelled as passengers in the train back to 'the Cross', while I was asked questions about the locomotive, this being my preliminary examination.

On 29 June 1956 I had my eight-hour examination with Chief Loco Inspector Harold Emery in an office adjacent to York Road Platform. After being given a cup of tea to relax me, I had a full day, first on all Rules & Regulations – and nothing was missed out – then, after a short break, the steam locomotive itself was covered: faults and failures and how to do temporary repairs; the vacuum, Westinghouse and steam brake systems, how they worked and correcting failures; the working of valves and pistons on

---

Extract from 'British Transport Commission Handbook for Railway Steam Locomotive Enginemen', 1957

EXAMINATIONS

A careful study of this Handbook will assist Firemen to become proficient in their duties and prepare them for their examination to pass as Drivers, which will be held on the following subjects…

The technical examination to act as Driver, which will be carried out by a Motive Power Inspector, will comprise an oral and practical examination:

(a) Oral Examination

The candidate to be examined in the following subjects:
1) Knowledge of locomotive
2) Knowledge of mechanism of continuous brakes
3) Method of dealing with locomotive defects
4) Knowledge of rules and regulations
5) Knowledge of the various types of signals, their use and the rules relating to the reading of signals

6) Knowledge of the making out of reports

(b) Practical Examinations

The Examiner will give attention to the following points:
1) Care and manipulation of locomotive
2) Attention to boiler and fire
3) Attention to signals and judging distances
4) Attention to rules and regulations
5) Knowledge of locomotive parts
6) Making and using trimmings
7) Care in and attention to oiling
8) Examining locomotive and reporting defects
9) General knowledge of automatic and steam brakes
10) Ability of examinee to change a boiler water gauge glass

These examinations will take place over a period of 2-3 days.

---

both two- and three-cylinder locomotives; and lubricating systems and how they all worked. Every single part of the steam locomotive was covered, and at the end of the day Inspector Emery informed me that I was now a driver, and after seeing the Inspector at Top Shed the next day, to complete any paperwork, 'sign the roads' over which I would be confident to drive, and be issued with various drivers' publications, I could then be booked out as a driver. That day I went home walking on air, knowing that I had now achieved my ambition to become a driver, and I would now be driving steam locomotives in my own right. So ended my eventful firing career.

5
A DRIVER AT LAST

On 30 June 1956 I started my first day's work as a 'Passed Fireman'; although I was now passed for driving duties, it could be possible for me to do firing duties if there was no driving duty to be covered. However, I was very lucky as, during my whole career as a 'Passed Fireman' (Spare Driver), never once did I go back to firing.

It was strange after so many years to be signing on duty on the left-hand side of the signing-on sheet – the 'driver's side' – while to the right of my name was my fireman's signature, who had already signed on for that day.

I was informed that I should go to the Loco Inspector's office before reporting to the shed foreman for instructions. The Inspector congratulated me on passing my examinations, and said that the first thing to do was to sign the route knowledge card, saying what routes I would be confident to drive. I therefore 'signed the road' (as it was called) from King's Cross to Doncaster on the main line and via Hertford North, as well as Hitchin to Cambridge and all the GN suburban routes, including freight yards and loco depots. I was then issued with all of the working timetables and many other publications covering the area where I would be driving. The Inspector then reminded me to collect the weekly working, which had to be signed for every week and gave details of all engineering work, altered speed restrictions and any other information applicable to the routes over which I would be working. In addition to this I was asked many questions about 'the road' over which I said that I was confident to drive – remember that I had fired over these routes for 13 years, which in my opinion was the best way to 'learn the road'. The Inspector then shook my hand and wished me good luck, and so began my first day as a Spare Driver.

I made my way to the messroom where my fireman was waiting for me, and we then walked over to the shed foreman's office. This was a narrow wooden building looking across the front of the main-line shed, where there was an assortment of 'V2', 'A1', 'A3' and 'A4' locos, and was where we reported for instructions. Our first job of the day was to prepare a Class 'J52', run 'light engine' to East Goods Yard on the up (east) side of the main line south of Finsbury Park station, and change over with the existing shunt pilot, which had been shunting there for more than 24 hours. It thus needed to return to Top Shed for coal and for the fire to be cleaned and the smokebox and ashpan to be emptied, as well as to be topped up with water – this would be a busy job for my fireman. The loco would then be ready for the fitters to check it for defects, then it would be ready for the next crew to prepare it for its next turn of duty.

Returning to where we had prepared the loco, we proceeded to the Loco outlet signal where my fireman told the signalman at Goods & Mineral Box, 'Light to East Goods Yard to change over Pilots.' We waited at the signal for a few minutes, then it was 'pulled off' for us to proceed. I must say that it was a strange feeling when I opened the regulator and the loco started to move. Here I was having achieved an ambition to drive a steam loco, albeit only a Class 'J52', in my own right, looking across the cab at the fireman whom I knew would be looking to me for any guidance; as for me, all decisions and responsibilities were mine. We eventually returned to the shed, having changed over locos at East Goods Yard, and had our meal break in the messroom.

We had barely finished our snack when the messroom telephone rang, and someone sitting nearby answered it. 'Driver Ruffell on the phone.' It was the shed foreman with instructions for us to go down to King's Cross Passenger and relieve on an arriving loco, then bring it to the shed. We therefore walked down to 'the Cross', and into platform 4 came an Edinburgh train with a Peppercorn 'A1' hauling it. The crew spoke to us with Geordie accents, and went off for their meal break.

As I sat in the driver's seat, waiting for the empty stock to be hauled away, I began to think about my first day as a driver – that morning it had been a 'J52', and now it was a Peppercorn 'A1' to drive up to Top Shed. My thoughts were suddenly brought to an abrupt halt by a father asking if his son could come up into the cab, to which I agreed. Of course Dad came as well, and they asked a few questions; the little boy was fascinated by it all, and eventually they went, thanking us for the experience. To be honest, I think it was the Dads who really enjoy coming on to the footplate, and it was nice to be in a position to give someone a little bit of pleasure.

The empty stock having been taken off to the sidings, I eased the regulator open and the 'A1' began to move down to the end of the platform, where we waited for the signal to take us through Gasworks Tunnel and on to Top Shed. There, in a small office located near the turntable, I reported any defects the loco had, these having been given to me by the Geordie crew. I then moved the loco on to the turntable, where it was turned by my fireman with the aid of the vacuum tractors, which were powered by the vacuum brake on the loco being turned. When turning a loco it

was important to open the cylinder cocks, apply the handbrake and put the reverser in mid-gear. We then moved the 'A1' to the coal stage, where we handed it over to another crew, who would be working on the shed.

That was the end of my first driving shift, and I was lucky to have a very conscientious 17-year-old fireman who was interested in the job, which was a great help to me. The only things left to do were to write out my Daily Driver's Ticket with my fireman's name, and all details of our day's work, and check the roster for my next day's turn of duty, as this could alter on a daily basis. As I walked down to 'the Cross' to catch my train home to Hornsey, I pondered that I had come a long way since I, and many of my friends, had gone trainspotting, mainly at Harringay, between 1940 and 1942. Another venue had been Tottenham Marshes, where we were able to observe the GE main line to Cambridge and King's Lynn, as well as the many freight trains bound for Whitemoor (March) and Temple Mills, between Stratford and Lea Bridge, not to mention our frequent visits to Neasden, Willesden, Old Oak Common and Cricklewood loco sheds, which were done on our bicycles. Now here I was, some 16 years later, as a loco driver, many a schoolboy's dream. On arrival at King's Cross I went to platform 15 for my train home, hauled by a Class 'N2' on the usual '2 x 4' articulated set.

Over the weeks I found myself getting into a routine, which mainly consisted of preparing locos and using gallons of oil. Some classes used more than others – it could take more than 20 pints to oil a 'Pacific'. We very often then took the loco down to 'the Cross', backing it on to its train and being relieved by another crew who would be working the train. We would then probably relieve a Top Shed crew on a train coming in from the north and take the loco to the shed. This did break up the continuous oiling of locos, allowing us to get away from the shed for short periods.

Most drivers had a spare set of overalls in their locker to be worn over their existing ones to protect them, so that if we went away from the shed, or travelled 'on the cushions', we could take the oily ones off before leaving the shed. Believe me, it was a very dirty job oiling a loco – going underneath into the pit and climbing up with one foot on each side of the pit to oil the 'motions'. Gresley three-cylinder locos were easy to oil due to the '2 to 1' lever – there would only be the middle big end and small end to oil – while the Peppercorn and Thompson 'Pacifics' had more motions underneath. Of course, inside-cylinder locos had all of the motions underneath. The easiest to oil were those with two outside cylinders and with the motions on the outside. To get access to the mechanical lubricator and lubrication boxes on the 'A4s' we used a ladder; this left us with both hands free, which made the job easier.

When it was dark, not only was there the oil-feeder, but also the flare lamp for illumination purposes; the latter was similar to a small oil-feeder but full of paraffin, and projecting from a short wide spout was a thick wick, which, when alight, provided illumination for any oiling. Of course it was even worse when it was pouring with rain or windy; when the wind blew out the flare lamp it had to be re-lit. Then, if a cork in the big end lubrication hole broke, it had to be dug out before it could be oiled; the wise driver always carried in his overall jacket spare corks, a small penknife, a box of matches and a couple of cloths. Another hazard while oiling underneath would be the fireman overfilling the tender with water; when it overflowed the water would run down the water scoop into the pit, so for safety reasons I always told my fireman when I was going under the loco to do any job, and hopefully he would remember that I was underneath and not overflow the tank. So as you can see there was a less glamorous side to a driver's job.

In addition to the normal shed work, such as moving locos under the coaling plant to be coaled, then running them on to the ashpit to have their fires cleaned (most of this work was done by the Top Shed fire-droppers), when locos had to be moved into the running sheds it was sometimes difficult due to their low steam pressure, so then the loco shed pilot, a Class 'J52', would be used to move them. This pilot would be the loco used to move any 'dead' locos in the shed or loco yard, or in and out of the workshops for heavy repairs.

I would also work on the shunt pilots in Kings Cross Goods Yard, freight transfer trips to all the yards – the furthest being Ferme Park – empty stock workings in and out of 'the Cross', and occasionally I would get a trip out to either Hertford North or Welwyn Garden City, which would be on a Class 'N2'. Then there would be the odd trip out on to the main line, working a freight or express train to either Peterborough, Grantham, Doncaster or Cambridge, but those sort of trips were few and far between! After several months, when I was due to re-sign my route card I had to cross out 'the road' to both Grantham and Doncaster, on the grounds that I had not had enough trips to either destination to keep acquainted with the route. This meant that before I could drive again to those two places I would require to have a refresher course over the road. I did, however, continue to sign the road to both Cambridge and Peterborough, as I was getting a few trips to both destinations.

By now the diesel locos were beginning to arrive and I found myself on a course to learn the 350hp shunters (later known as Class 08). During 1956 I was trained on English Electric, BTH Blackstone and GEC diesel-electrics, which were rapidly replacing the 'J52s' on shunting duties and local freight transfer trips. I must say that I enjoyed the comfort of the cab compared with a 'J52', but it took a long time when working in the yard to get used to being alone in the cab, as no fireman was required; this would be the beginning of a lonely job with no mate to converse with. These shunters could be driven from either side of the cab as they had dual controls; however, a fireman was still required if the loco was to go out on a running line.

After being on steam for so many years, it took time to get used to the diesels. One good thing, which took a little time to get used to, was going home clean. The one thing I disliked was the smell of the diesel fumes; sometimes, depending on the weather conditions, while looking out of the cab during a shunting movement the exhaust would come downwards, making it very unpleasant. Also, in a tunnel the fumes persisted – had it been steam and smoke from a steam loco it would have dispersed quickly.

The first 350hp locos I worked on were brand new and painted black. Later more of these locos were allocated to Top Shed, but we now had a change of colour as they were painted in BR green and carried what I call the 'starved lion' BR crest.

I recall working with one of the black-liveried locos for a full week in the yard at Highbury Vale, and on the Saturday afternoon my instructions were to stable the loco in the coal yard, isolate the electrics, lock the doors and check the fuel in the main tank, the idea being that the loco would already be in the yard to start work on Monday morning, and I would not have to take it to Top Shed, which would save 'light engine' running. However, I still had to make my way to Top Shed to book off duty and report to the foreman how much fuel the '350' had remaining in its tank. The end of this little story is that when the driver arrived at Highbury Vale to mobilise the '350' on Monday morning, somebody had been in the coal yard over the weekend and emptied the main tank of its diesel fuel, which to my knowledge was never seen again.

Then to my surprise I was booked to have some instruction on a Drewry 204hp diesel-mechanical shunter, one of which had been sent to King's Cross to see how it would perform in the Goods Yard. Having reported to the Loco Inspector's office, where the Diesel Instructor was waiting for me, we made our way to the Goods Yard to join the driver on the Drewry. I was given some paperwork all about the loco, and practical experience with the driver shunting in the yard. I worked on this loco for a few days with the driver, but I was not very impressed with its performance compared with the '350'. There was a great deal of difference in the horsepower, and it was heavy work in the Goods Yard – these locos did not appear suitable for the shunting involved. Far better to use a diesel-electric loco where no gear-changing was involved. It was not very long before the Drewry was transferred away to another depot, and it would be a few years before I would set foot on one again.

Being a driver mainly doing shed work did tend to get monotonous. Rarely did I get the same fireman two days running, and while

350hp diesel-electric shunter No 13308, new in May 1956 and later numbered D3308, is seen at Highbury Vale when brand new. Withdrawn in 1984, the loco was subsequently preserved.

Sister shunter No 13331 (later D3331) is seen in King's Cross Goods Yard in 1957, where I was photographed at the controls.

some of them were very good, others had no interest in the job at all. To the latter it was simply a job, but the shift work usually got the better of them and they left for other employment. Many of those who were interested did stay over the years, some of them becoming drivers.

On 20 April 1958 I was appointed a 'Regular Driver', which meant that I would be on the driver's side of the roster and would also have the same fireman rostered with me. We are now rostered in the link doing mainly local goods work, but should a senior link job need to be covered (due to holidays or sickness) I would be booked to cover it. This also meant that I could not be put back as a fireman.

As some of the work I would be covering was freight diagrams going to High Barnet, Mill Hill and Edgware, I was booked out for road-learning, all of this work being done at that time by our faithful 'N2' Class. I did a great deal of work to all three of those places, and what made it more interesting was running over Northern Line metals from East Finchley. In general the trips were without problems. However, on one occasion my mate and I travelled passenger to Highbury Vale from Top Shed to relieve another crew who had already worked two trips to the gas works without any problems, but we were to have an unpleasant experience with the 'N2' on a train of coal going to Mill Hill Gas Works Sidings. We successfully accomplished one round trip from Highbury Vale, going up with a train of coal and returning with the empties, and it was now time to depart with our second trip. Having propelled our train of coal out of the sidings on to the running line, we were ready to go; we 'had the road' (the signals were clear) so I opened the regulator, my mate got busy on the shovel, and off we went uphill nearly all the way from Highbury Vale to East Finchley.

Emerging from the tunnel at Highgate the road levelled out on the approach to East Finchley, and on this occasion there were no Northern Line trains due so we had all green lights. I opened the regulator and off we went through East Finchley, then it was a fairly level road until the approach to Finchley Central, where it was a slightly falling gradient. By this time I was braking, with yellow signals ahead, but I was getting very little response from the brake – remember that the 'N2' only had a vacuum brake, and my train of coal was loose-coupled, so it was solely the loco's brake that kept the train under control. By this time we were doing a series of 'pop' whistles to attract the attention of our guard to assist us by screwing down his handbrake in the guard's van. With the small amount of brake power on the loco, and the assistance from the guard, we gradually began to slow down. Ahead was a red signal, which we passed. Finchley Central was a junction, so all sorts of things were going through my mind if we were unable to stop. We now passed another red signal as we slowed down, and just as we passed the signal box on the approach to the station we came to a stop with the brake fully applied, sanders open, and the loco in reverse.

I was shaking like a leaf – God knows what this had done to my blood pressure – but I was so thankful that we had not caused an accident. My fireman gave me every assistance and said that it would be something he would remember for the rest of his life. Believe me, he was not alone in thinking this!

After consultation with the signalman, London Transport Control and our own Control, we were able to clear the Northern Line by slowly shunting our train into a siding, where we 'scotched' the loco to stop it moving and pinned down some wagon brakes. On examining the loco's brake gear we found that all of the locking nuts on the adjusting rods were loose, and with oil and grease on the threads, together with the vibration, all of the adjusting nuts were working loose, making the brake useless. Obviously somebody who had done some maintenance on the loco in the shed had slipped up.

We rounded off our day with another 'N2' coming 'light engine' from Top Shed accompanied by a fitter to examine our loco. After some discussion the two 'N2s' were coupled together and we were towed to the shed, leaving our train of coal in the siding at Finchley Central. On arrival at the shed our loco was immediately placed over a pit for examination, and before I could book off duty I had to submit a full report about the incident, which would be the end of our involvement in the affair.

Between 1956 and 1961 so many things happened. In early 1959 six of us drivers were sent to the Training School at Ilford to attend a diesel instruction course. This involved lots of writing, lectures and tests, then we had a week out driving on an 1160hp Birmingham RC&W/Sulzer Type 2 diesel-electric loco. This also included all of the 'faults and failures' that we were expected to be able to correct. After a total of three weeks' instruction, both in the classroom and on the loco, we were tested on our knowledge and the handling of the loco in service, and I am pleased to say that all six of us passed. Once again, as with the 350hp shunters, I enjoyed the comfort of the cab and going home clean, but I found the smell of diesel very unpleasant. Driving a diesel loco needed some getting used to as the cab was at the front, and from my point of view, after spending 25 years on steam, I was used to looking along the full

length of the boiler from a side-window cab; at first, therefore, judging braking distances when approaching signals and buffer stops needed a slightly different technique.

I now found myself working back on steam and enjoying the company of my fireman, doing the occasional day preparing locos on the shed. I recall on one of these days that we were given an 'A4' to prepare for the 10am out of 'the Cross' (the 'Flying Scotsman'). The Top Link driver was 65 years old on that day, and this would be his last trip as he had reached retiring age and would be finished with the footplate. We prepared the 'A4' and my fireman put the 'Flying Scotsman' headboard on the front. Dick Ball and his gang of cleaners had done a good job – the 'A4' was spotless, and a credit to him and his gang.

Driver John Brown and his fireman duly arrived to take charge of the 'A4', which they would be working on the 'Scotsman' to Grantham. They would then go 'light engine' to Grantham Loco and work another express back to 'the Cross' in the early afternoon. I

In early 1959 I was trained to drive the 1160hp Birmingham RC&W/Sulzer Type 2 diesel-electric locos (later Class 26). An example is seen here at speed on the East Coast Main line neat Hatfield in 1958.

Back on steam, my fireman used my camera to take this picture of me at the controls of 'A4' No 60010 *Dominion of Canada* leaving Top Shed in 1957.

had a chat with him, saying that the loco was all prepared and all he had to do was sit in the chair and open the regulator. He told me that his life was steam and that he had enjoyed his career and was very unhappy about retiring, which I felt was very sad. However, it was now time for him to leave the shed, and I shook hands with him, wishing him all the best for the future and hoping that he had a good round trip. He then got on the 'A4' and a group of us saw him off the shed.

I am sorry to say that this little story has a sad ending. A few weeks later we were very surprised to hear that John had passed away. I and many others were shocked at his early death, and after that conversation I had with him my feelings are that he died of a broken heart.

Over the months I found myself doing an assortment of jobs, much of it empty stock work and shunt pilot at King's Cross Passenger. The spur where our loco stood while waiting to make a shunt was just outside the entrance to Gasworks Tunnel, and while it was a good vantage point to observe the activity of trains departing and arriving, the snag was that every time an express entered the tunnel we got the full benefit of the smoke as it billowed out – of course it was even worse on a wet day. Some days our loco would be an 'N2', other days an 'L1', and often we would work empty stock to either Bounds Green or

Above When working as shunt pilot at King's Cross Passenger, the spur where our loco stood, just outside Gasworks Tunnel, was a good vantage point to observe trains departing and arriving. Back in 1947 this was the view from an 'N1' 0-6-2T of the station 'throat' and the main-line platforms, with the suburban station on the right.

Right An 'A4' being turned on the turntable at King's Cross in 1947.

Hornsey Carriage Sidings, or be coupled on to a suburban set to work a passenger train to either Welwyn Garden City or Hertford North.

On one occasion we were on a shed duty job, with instructions to relieve on an express at 'the Cross'. It came in with a 'V2' on it, and we waited for a considerable time for the empty stock to go. Eventually it went, and we drew down to the end of the platform to wait for our signal to take us to Top Shed. Imagine my surprise when an Inspector came over to me asking if I would work some empty stock to Hornsey Sidings, as there was a problem with the loco that was booked to work it. There was no other loco available, and they needed to clear the platform. After some consultation with my fireman (as it was going to involve us working a lot of overtime) we agreed to do the work.

We were coupled on to 12 cars, and my fireman got busy on the shovel, getting the

'A2' No 60530 *Sayajirao* leaves with an express – notes that the steam sanders are operating, to aid adhesion with the heavy train up through Gasworks Tunnel.

Staff on the ground speak to the crews of an 'L1' 2-6-4T and a 'B17' 4-6-0 couple together.

steam pressure to just over 200psi (bearing in mind that both the fire and pressure had been kept down for disposal purposes on arrival at the shed). Having had a word with our guard, we now 'had the road' so I opened the regulator and off we went. This was the first time I had ever worked a train out of 'the Cross' tender-first, and I have to say that it felt strange, but the 'V2' made easy work of it. It was a pity that there were no photographers around as it would have made a good picture climbing the bank to Holloway North – after all, we would normally have had either an 'N2' or 'L1'. On our arrival at Bounds Green we ran round the train, put it through the washing plant, then worked the stock to Hornsey Carriage Sidings, where we were uncoupled, taking the 'V2' 'light engine' to Top Shed. I was not a person who enjoyed working overtime, but

I must say I enjoyed doing this trip as it was 'different'.

It was now back to the classroom at Ilford School to be trained on the 1,000hp North British/MAN Type 2 D61xx diesel-electric locos, ten of which were to be based at 'the Cross', and I was to do a great deal of work on them. I must say that I preferred to work on the Birmingham RC&W/Sulzers, as we experienced a lot of trouble with the MAN diesel engine.

During this period I was doing a lot of work with both types of diesel loco on all suburban routes, as well as on the Cambridge trains. One particular diagram I worked many times was a late-afternoon job that consisted of working a semi-fast from 'the Cross' down to Cambridge, where we had our meal break, then going light to the goods yard and working a loose-coupled freight train back to Hitchin.

The first time I saw a Type 4 English Electric 2,000hp diesel-electric loco (later Class 40) was at Hornsey shed, and I recall reading in the local paper (the *Hornsey Journal*) that the first 'Green Goddess' locomotive had arrived at Hornsey, which heralded the beginning of the end for steam.

I was now in the process of planning another holiday in Norway, going by train from Hook of Holland to Oslo, then into the Arctic Circle to Saltdal (in 1957 this was the end of the line), bus to Bodo, then on the coastal boat to Kirkenes via the Lofoten Isles and North Cape. It was a great trip and took 3½ weeks, giving me many memories. To round off the trip I had the privilege of riding in the cab of a General Motors diesel-electric loco from Copenhagen to Gedser; the driver, who spoke fluent English, made this part of the trip extremely interesting, and the locos were new, having just put into service.

Back to work, I was soon back to the steam/diesel routines, sometimes working on steam, sometimes on diesels – we now called ourselves 'dual drivers'. I recall doing a full week's work on a loose-coupled freight from Highbury Vale to Hitchin, train number 1234. The return working from Hitchin was 'as required', which meant that if there was no train for us to work back, we would travel home 'on the cushions'. However, Control usually managed to produce a train for us to work, anything from a parcels train to a slow freight. The loco I was allocated to work 1234 from Highbury Vale was a BR Standard 9F 2-10-0. This was the only BR Standard class that I worked on, and I must say as a driver that the 9F was a good loco to handle and was master of any load or type of train, and comfortable to work on. I did many trips on this class, enjoying them all. The only other Standard locos I recall seeing on the GN were the 'Britannias' that worked the 4.10pm from King's Cross to Cleethorpes (a working that was taken over from 'B1s'), and sometimes a Standard Class 5 would work a Cambridge train, probably with a Cambridge crew.

One foggy Saturday morning my fireman and I were booked on shed duty, and on reporting to the shed foreman for orders we were told to prepare a 'B1' and go 'light engine' to Western Sidings, pick up our train and work a semi-fast from Finsbury Park to Cambridge. The fog was so dense that we could just about see the front of the loco. It was a very unpleasant trip, but by the time we reached Royston the fog was clearing, and on arrival at Cambridge out came the sun. After my mate unhooked our loco, we went 'light engine' to the depot to turn and water, and could then brew a can of tea and have a bite to eat. The return trip to 'the Cross' would be faster, as we would be working a 'Buffet Express' calling at Royston, Hitchin and Welwyn Garden City. The 'B1' made easy work of the train, but it was due for a major overhaul at the 'Plant', and at high speeds we had to stand up due to the rough ride! On arrival at London we were relieved by a Top Shed crew, and went home with the sound of the valve gear and side rods ringing in our ears.

Once again it was back to the classroom to learn all about the Cravens diesel multiple units (DMUs), which were to take over the GN suburban service. After a week in the classroom on the theory, we went out on the road with a two-car unit to learn the practical side of them, including all faults and failures, on a non-service train. This took several more days, then there would be an examination to see if we were proficient. On my first trip with a service train a Loco Inspector would be riding in the cab with me.

From our point of view a problem had developed as to where we were to sign on duty. Although Top Shed was our depot, we now found ourselves signing on duty at either Top Shed, King's Cross Passenger or Finsbury Park station, and to the best of my recollection there was no travelling-time allowance. Consequently this new system did not go down very well with the staff, as over the course of a week you could be signing on at three different locations. Nevertheless, management in their wisdom implemented the new system, with many drivers like myself being put to a great deal of inconvenience; as most of our equipment was in our lockers at Top Shed, this also created problems!

The first day that Cravens DMUs took over

most of the GN suburban service I signed on duty at Finsbury Park in the late afternoon, and 20 minutes later I was driving a DMU in passenger service into Moorgate. I was on my own, as there was no Loco Inspector to ride with me. I did not enjoy this first trip, first because it was all new to me, and second because of the glass panels and door separating the cab from the passenger section, which meant that many passengers stood at the front watching every move the driver made. I was not keen on having an audience watching me work, and felt a lot happier when back on a diesel or steam loco.

Returning to steam, at about this period there was a great deal of PW engineering work taking place at weekends between Wood Green and Hatfield, so trains were being diverted via Hertford North. Signing on duty at Top Shed on a Saturday night, I was booked to pilot a Doncaster crew on a No 1-speed 'fitted' freight from King's Cross Goods Yard to New England North – this was because the Doncaster driver did not have the 'road knowledge'. Having arrived at New England North, I walked through the yards to Eastfield signal box where I waited for my next working, to pilot another Doncaster crew to King's Cross Goods Yard. Over the months I was to do these trips several times, and the locos I drove were always 'V2s'; it was a great feeling to be in charge of this class of loco. After all, it had taken many years of hard work, but sadly the writing was on the wall, and what I enjoyed doing most of all was to disappear at some future date. The 'N2s' were being replaced by DMUs, and the 'B1s' and 'L1s' were being replaced by diesel locos; even some of the main-line expresses were being hauled by diesels, so to me the railway that I had been brought up with was slowly disappearing, and we were having to learn many new skills. The only thing that appeared to us to be missing was any financial reward for all this extra knowledge and the number of diesel locomotives we had been trained to work on. Of course there were also alterations to the Rule Book due to single-manning, which we had to keep up to date with, together with the various other publications for the safe running of trains with the

introduction of single-manning, this being done in our own time.

Then once again it was back to the classroom with three other drivers, this time to be trained on the 1,365hp Brush Type 2/3 diesel-electric locos. At the end of the training period there was another oral and practical test on all the faults and failures of the loco, then it was out on the road to see how we handled them. All four of us passed, so we could now go out on the road with yet another class of loco. I must say that I was very impressed with these engines – their performance was good and they were a comfortable loco to work on. The first one I worked on was No D5666, and these locos later became Class 31. They were used on every form of train from empty stock to stopping and semi-fast workings, and imagine my surprise when, on looking at the roster for the following week's work, I found that I was booked on a new diagram that involved me working two round trips from King's Cross to Cambridge. This was something new, as with a steam loco all we did was one round trip. Imagine the operating costs that this must have saved. I must say it was strange at first, after having worked one trip and taken a short meal break, to leave 'the Cross' again on a second trip.

One Saturday night shift we were booked on engineering work in Gasworks Tunnel. Being in the tunnel was bad enough, but having to put up with all the fumes from the bulldozers and other machinery in use was worse, together with the exhaust from our Brush loco when we moved the spoil wagons along. We were standing on the slow line, with track being removed on Main 2; all the ballast was being removed, and we understood that something was also being done to the drainage system. After 8 hours of this we were relieved, and for some days all we could smell and taste was diesel – not very good for our health. To this day I do not know how the men working at ground level could stand the conditions. Both my fireman and myself agreed it was one of the worst night's work we had experienced.

During 1959 I and my fiancée had a holiday in Wales on my LE 'Velocette', a shaft-driven, water-cooled 200cc bike. Of course visits had to made to the narrow gauge railways, and imagine my pleasure on Porthmadog station when I met a former colleague, Allan Garraway. We had not met for many years, not since he was the AWS Inspector at 'the Cross', and he immediately invited me to ride on the footplate from Porthmadog to Tan-y-Bwlch and back on one of the famous Fairlie locos. Then came an even bigger surprise – the driver was Jim Maxwell, who I had also not seen for many years, not since the days when I used to drive his live-steam Armstrong 0-6-0 goods loco at various model railway shows. So a very enjoyable day was had by all – my fiancée assured me that she did not mind me riding on the footplate, and that I should enjoy it. I must say that it was a great experience, and great to meet old friends, although I did feel a little guilty about my fiancée riding in the train on her own, but then I was not far away!

The Class 'N2s' were still being used on all of the freight trains to High Barnet, Edgware and Mill Hill, but their days were numbered. I must have been one of the last group of drivers to work these trains with steam, because, yes, once again it was back to the classroom to take a course on the BTH/Paxman 800hp Type 1 D82xx diesel-electric loco. This time the course was for one week, which included the usual theory, faults and failures, handling the loco out on the road (with loose-coupled trains), and at the end of it all a theory and practical test. Needless to say, our group all passed, so now we would be using these locos to run over London Transport metals; they were fitted with 'trip gear' to comply with LT signalling regulations. I must say it felt strange on my first trip with a diesel, but they did perform very well on these freight workings.

I had now been trained and passed to drive a total of eight different types of diesel locos; add to this the Craven DMUs, and we were also working on steam locos, so life was very hectic. With the business of signing on duty at three different locations, as you can probably realise we were not a very happy workforce.

However, that year I would be having a two-week break from all of this chaos, getting married, and spending two weeks in Switzerland away from it all. I must say that I never gave the Eastern Region of British Railways a single thought!

I had for many years considered myself an enthusiastic railwayman, but I am afraid that, in my eyes, things were changing for the worse. First, I was not very keen working on diesel locomotives, possible because I had to learn so much over a fairly short period, and second, my biggest interest was steam locomotives, and these were to disappear, leaving me just the diesel locos. It is easy to understand why so many drivers and firemen decided to leave railway service with the phasing out of steam and the introduction of diesels. This was the time when many enthusiastic footplate staff changed their occupations, and in my opinion it was sad to see so many people leave the industry.

As for myself, I decided to stick it out in the hope that things would improve. It was not only the loss of steam, but also a slow erosion of our conditions of service – but that is a long story that I intend to cover later. Meanwhile I had no time to get bored – we appeared to be 'Jacks of all trades', with a mixture of every form of traction to be driven on everything from a main-line train to a slow freight, yard shunting, working DMUs, and still some steam work. There were also still times when I found myself at Top Shed preparing steam locos of any class from 'A1' down to the 'L1' 2-6-4T.

At about this time my wife and I had the opportunity to move into a brand new house at Ware in East Hertfordshire, and as there was a depot at Hertford East it seemed a good idea to apply for a transfer. This would mean working on the old GE section, and after nearly 20 years on the GN section this needed a lot of thinking about. Hertford East depot only really consisted of a signing-on point with staff facilities, as the steam shed, turntable and other facilities had now been demolished; steam had gone, and in its place were electric and diesel multiple unit (EMU and DMU) workings, diesel loco workings on both parcel and freight trains, and a Saturday working on the Shunt Pilot at Ware. After discussions with my wife we decided that it would be a good idea to live at Ware and work at Hertford, as it was only 2-3 miles to travel to work, the shifts were better, with no shifts between 10pm and 4am and only two night shifts, with approximately 30 drivers based at the depot. It would mean that I would be turning my back on main-line work, as Hertford East mainly consisted of suburban workings, so after balancing all the pros and cons, we decided that we would probably enjoy a better social life, away from the erratic shift work and present workings at Top Shed. I therefore decided to take the plunge and apply for a transfer, knowing that it could be a long time coming, as I would have to wait for a vacancy.

While I waited I did a lot of empty coach workings and shunt pilots at King's Cross with Class 'L1' tanks, which, as I have already said, were not one of my favourite classes to work on. Also, with the introduction of diesel locos the maintenance of steam locos left a lot to be

desired, and with some of the steam leaks they were not very good for the health. Several months went by with our conditions being further eroded, and the inconvenience of signing on at three different locations was terrible, bearing in mind that this could happen during a single week's work. Travelling home to Ware daily – my choice, admittedly – coupled with shift work made life a nightmare.

Then, when I signed on at Top Shed on Wednesday 8 March 1961, I was handed a letter to say that there was a vacancy at Hertford East, and that I was to report there for duty on Monday the 13th at 9am, which gave me very little notice. My move was called an '8c', and was not advertised on the usual vacancy lists. So my last day as a driver at Top Shed was on Friday 10 March on a Class 'L1' 2-6-4T working an empty coach diagram, and getting relieved at King's Cross Passenger.

6
HERTFORD EAST

On Monday 13 March 1961, as I rode my LE 'Velocette' from Ware to Hertford on a cool but sunny morning, I could not help but wonder what the future would hold for me. The first good thing was it took me less than a quarter of an hour to get to the depot. The loco office and staff facilities were still located at the loco shed site, and I was greeted with a cup of tea by Bert Neve, who appeared to be the timekeeper. He dealt with rosters and issued weekly workings and timetables – in other words, ran the depot. He was assisted by George Phillips, who issued drivers' equipment and was responsible for the depot's stores, then once a week Mr Andrews, a motive power supervisor, came down from Stratford to check that everything was running smoothly.

When I left Top Shed I handed in all the publications and equipment connected with the GN section, so now I would be issued with everything applying to the GE section. I was

Me and my trusty LE 'Velocette', with Welwyn Viaduct in the background.

Hertford East station in much later Network SouthEast days, 13 August 1989.

also given the following list of roads that I would have to learn:

1 Hertford East-Liverpool Street via the Lee Valley and Southbury Loop
2 Broxbourne-Audley End via Bishops Stortford
3 St Margarets-Buntingford
4 Edmonton Junction-Angel Road
5 Copper Mills Junction-Liverpool Street via Temple Mills and Stratford
6 Temple Mills Yard and Loco Depot
7 Stratford Diesel Depot
8 Billet Sidings (at High Meads, Stratford)

The first roads I should learn would be all of the electrified routes, over which Hertford East crews were at present running, and the branch line from St Margarets to Buntingford.

Having been issued with all of my publications, equipment and a locker, I received a phone call from Loco Inspector Elmer at Stratford, who wanted to know what types of diesel locos and DMUs I had been trained on. Having taken the details, he said that at some early date he would make arrangements for me to be trained first on the

EMUs and Rolls-Royce DMUs, then on the following diesel locos: Andrew Barclay 153hp diesel-mechanical; NBL/GEC 800hp diesel-electric (D84xx); and Brush/Mirrlees 1,250hp diesel-electric (Class 31). To start with I would learn the road over the Buntingford branch, then concentrate on the electrified routes, and in the meantime Mr Elmer would make arrangements for me to attend the three-week Electric Traction Course that was to be held at Southend. So, after a visit to the signal box to get some idea of what yard movements were made, and the procedure for washing units (there was a carriage cleaning plant located between the signal box and the site of the demolished steam shed), I then had a walk round the yard and station, observing where the running and subsidiary signals were positioned, and that ended my first day's work at Hertford East. Many months of traction training and road learning lay ahead.

On my second 15-minute journey motorcycling to work I found myself reflecting on the inconvenience that I had experienced during the few weeks that I had been travelling between Ware and King's Cross. Having moved house before the vacancy

The platforms at Hertford East in October 1984.

arose, I used to motorcycle to Hertford North then travel by train to King's Cross. This may sound a straightforward journey, but with erratic shift work and very few trains between midnight and 6am it could mean finishing a shift at 2am then having to wait for the next train at 4.45, so it would be about 6.15 before I got home. This had meant being away from home for about 14 hours to do an 8-hour shift. The reverse happened when I was on duty in the early hours of the morning (between midnight and 6am), and had to travel on the last train from Hertford North, then kill time at 'the Cross' for a few hours before signing on

duty at, say, 3.50am. So once again I was spending more time away from my home than actually in it, which does illustrate the problems for shift workers when travelling by public transport during the early 1960s. I am just grateful that I only had to do it for a few weeks before getting my transfer.

Signing on duty, I was given a pass to travel over the routes that I had to learn, so, having made my way to St Margarets station, I made my first trip to Buntingford on a Rolls-Royce DMU. I was very impressed with the unit's performance compared with the Cravens on which I had worked out of 'the Cross'. I was

One of the locos on which I would train at my new depot: Andrew Barclay 153hp diesel-mechanical shunter No 2956 is seen at Hertford East in the summer of 1964.

Above A Rolls-Royce DMU at Buntingford in 1964, with guard Mr Edwards.

Below GE Outer Suburban four-car unit No 510 (later Class 305) leaves Hertford East in the spring of 1964.

also very impressed with the scenic beauty of the branch, and felt that I would enjoy working over it in the future.

I now turned my attention to learning the roads that were 'wired' (Hertford East-Liverpool Street via the Southbury Loop, and Broxbourne-Bishops Stortford). This took many weeks, as it also involved Liverpool Street station itself. In the middle of all this I attended a three-week course at Southend to learn the EMUs. After a week in the classroom we had practical training out on the road with a unit that was not in public service, and at the end of all this we were tested on our knowledge and the 'faults and failures' of the EMUs, then had a practical trip on a service train with a Loco Inspector and driver. Having passed all this I was now qualified to drive the English Electric units that later became Classes 302 and 305, and the GEC Class 305 units.

Then it was off to Stratford for a conversion course to learn the Rolls-Royce DMUs, bearing in mind that I had already done the full DMU course while at King's Cross. At the end of the week it was a further test on 'faults and failures', then a practical test out on the road.

By now it was summer, so from my point of view it was a good time of the year to sign my route card, signifying that I was confident to drive over the routes that I had learned. Now I could start my driving career at Hertford East, and it was very strange at first as I had never fired over any of the roads, but after a few weeks I soon got the feel of it. However, there were problems as the EMUs proved to be unreliable, frequently failing and causing a great deal of delays; this was no help to me, being new to both the units and the road.

The main cause of the trouble was the units' dual-voltage system, which operated on either 6.25kV or 25kV. For example, between Theobalds Grove and Cheshunt, coming off the Southbury Loop, there was a neutral (dead) section between the two voltages, and it was at these sections that a lot of trouble was caused by the EMU's 'supply changeover switch' not functioning correctly. This switch was fed through an air-blast circuit-breaker, then to the main transformer, and specially designed equipment ensured that the transformer connections were the correct voltage before the air-blast circuit-breaker closed.

There were many other reasons why these EMUs failed. Sometimes we were able to correct the fault and carry on to our destination, but if not it would be a case of waiting for another train to couple on at the rear and push us to a convenient station where the defective unit could be taken out of service, all this after the various Rules & Regulations had been carried out. For many months there was a fitter based at Broxbourne to assist on any EMU that was a failure.

The roster structure worked at Hertford consisted of two links: No 1 was all EMU work, while No 2 was DMU, EMU and diesel loco workings. Both links had a small number of 'as required' turns of duty, to cover holidays, sickness and leave, and there was just one night shift: the first passenger train to leave Hertford East was at 4.25am. I was rostered in No 2 link, which is why so many roads needed to be learned. One of the diagrams was working a loose-coupled freight train from Hertford to Temple Mills, picking up at some of the yards along the Lea Valley; at this period all the stations along the valley had a yard that was shunted daily. On arrival at Temple Mills we went 'light engine' either to the 'Mills' depot or Stratford diesel depot. There was also a parcels train from Hertford worked by Hertford crews, which called at various stations along the Lea Valley, finishing up at Liverpool Street, where relief was by a Stratford crew.

I now found myself on another course to be trained on both the NBL/GEC 800hp diesel-electric loco and the Andrew Barclay 153hp diesel-mechanical shunter. Successfully passing the tests on both of these locos, it was time to learn the road along the Lea Valley (Cheshunt-Stratford-Clapton Junction-Temple Mills Yard and loco depot), where the passenger service was operated by Rolls-Royce DMUs. The Lea Valley was a busy section of line, with four tracks running from Pickett's Lock right through to Temple Mills Yard (two of them classed as goods roads), with the majority of the signalling being semaphore signals. Many

Another diesel-electric loco on which I trained was the NBL/GEC 800hp Type 1 Bo-Bo. Only 10 were built, and No D8406 is seen at Hertford East in the summer of 1964.

of the yards had a daily shunting pilot, and over a long period Hertford crews were utilised on these pilots at either Ponders End, Brimsdown or Waltham Cross, being relieved by Stratford crews.

Between learning all these roads, I was also working my own rostered EMU diagrams, which helped to break up the road learning. It took a long time to learn Temple Mills Yard, but after many visits it did all click into place, and eventually I signed the route card to the effect that I was now confident to drive over all of these roads.

While gaining all of this knowledge I found myself on a course to be trained on the units that were to become Class 308. It was now getting towards the end of 1962, and just as Christmas arrived it began to snow heavily and became very cold. For many days there was no sign of the weather improving; in fact, it got worse with blizzards, frost and ice, and temperatures going down to many degrees below freezing. These conditions carried on over the whole of the British Isles for about eight weeks, then when the thaw came so did the floods, which lasted for another 3-4 weeks. This turned out to be the worst winter since 1740, with the coldest month being January.

The problems this created on the railways were horrific. In the first place it was very difficult to get to work, the snow being so deep – there were no buses running, but we were expected to get to the depot early in the morning to attempt to start some form of train service. The only way I could get there, like

many other people, was to walk, and when I did eventually arrive at the depot there were more problems with the EMUs and DMUs being frozen up.

Due to the weather conditions an extra driver was booked to work on nights, and the two drivers checked the units all night as follows:

1 All the pantographs were to be kept up, lowering and raising them occasionally to avoid icing up, as the weight of any ice would force the pantograph down; also, leaving the pantograph up would keep the unit's heating and auxiliary systems in operation.
2 Braking systems were to be operated through the night to avoid freezing up.
3 DMU engines were to be kept running all night, and all braking and heating systems checked.

For the two drivers on this duty it was a nightmare working under these conditions. During blizzards so much snow and ice built up on the pantographs that the weight lowered them just slightly, causing vivid arcing from the 25,000 volts as they jumped from the overhead wire to the 'pan'. This could both damage the overhead wires and the carbon on the 'pan', so the latter had to be dropped, which meant that the EMU and its systems would then freeze up, making it a failure for the morning service, unless the drivers were successful in getting the 'pan' back up. By this time the drivers would also be frozen and adjourned to the staff room to thaw out before going out again into the Arctic conditions to help ensure that at least some of the units would be able to start the morning service.

While working one of these night shifts, we had an instruction at 1am to work a unit to Cheshunt to assist a failed unit between the neutral section and Theobalds Grove station. With another driver and a guard, off we went to Cheshunt, where we were cautioned by the signalman and instructed to proceed on to the Southbury Loop. We were now looking for the guard from the failed unit who had carried out protection duties, and were suddenly confronted by a red light being waved. I automatically made a full brake application and we came to an abrupt stop. And where had we stopped? In the neutral section, so we too were now a failure, and would need assistance to clear the section. After trudging through a foot of snow to the nearest signal, I reported the situation to the signalman, saying that our guard was now walking back to protect our train and would arrive at Cheshunt box.

To cut a long story short, a March to Temple Mills freight train was stopped in Cheshunt station, the diesel loco was uncoupled, and our guard piloted the March driver to the rear of our failed unit. Eventually our unit was propelled out of the neutral section and under the live overhead wires, which of course made it fully operational. The diesel loco was uncoupled, then had to rejoin its train – but that, as they say, is another story! We then coupled on to the failed unit and propelled it to Liverpool Street, where we left it, working our unit 'empty stock' back to Hertford East, arriving at 5.30am. Even after arriving home it was hours before I thawed out – it was an experience not to be repeated.

Over the weeks there were several instances where the pantographs of units in service were coming down, caused once again by the weight of snow and ice. The train was then stopped by the driver under the protection of signals, and he had to ask for assistance as the unit was a failure. In a short time the train, passengers and crew would become very cold, because with the 'pan' down there would be no heaters, and it could be a long wait for an assisting train to be attached to the rear.

There was also an occasional problem with points freezing up, although they were fitted with gas heaters at Copper Mills Junction. The Lea Valley service, being operated by DMUs, was therefore sometimes diverted to Liverpool Street via Stratford instead of Hackney Downs.

Working the DMUs could be a cold job. I sometimes had to drive them wearing overcoat, gloves and scarf, together with wool-lined boots, because the heaters had failed due to the diesel fuel freezing. On two occasions I was forced by the severe cold in the cab to fail the unit on arrival at Broxbourne; in my opinion it would have been unsafe to carry on due to the difficulty of concentrating due to the cold. There were some cases when the temperature went well below zero and the diesel fuel actually froze in the fuel tank, so there were more failures.

One highlight I do remember well was one morning after a night of blizzards, when working the first train from St Margarets to Buntingford. Running ahead of me was the snowplough, and the countryside was a picturesque sight with thick snow everywhere. This was a scenic branch during the summer, but I felt it was a privilege to see it under these conditions – the landscape was beautiful. On arrival at Buntingford I found the platform packed with passengers – all the roads in this part of Hertfordshire were impassable due to the excessive snowfall. It went through my mind that if this number of people used the trains on a permanent basis there would never be any fear of the branch closing.

Once again we followed the snowplough back to St Margarets, and at every station we picked up more and more passengers. By the time we reached Hadham our three-car DMU was full to capacity, and at Widford and Mardock passengers had difficulty in boarding. Eventually we arrived at St Margarets a few minutes late, due to the thickness of the snow in two of the cuttings where it had drifted, together with the large number of passengers. One of the highlights of this particular trip was leaving Standon and seeing a fox running in the snow parallel with our train for about a quarter of a mile. It really was a wonderful sight – if only it could have been filmed.

Everyone was pleased to see the back of that winter and welcomed the spring. During that summer I was involved in an incident on the approach to Spellbrook while working an empty EMU from Liverpool Street to Bishops Stortford. Travelling at 70mph my unit suddenly lost all power, and ahead what appeared to be a ball of fire rose into the air. As we went round the bend approaching the Spellbrook Loop, I realised that something was very wrong. I had already applied the emergency brake, and to my horror I could now see a large tree stretching from the railway bank and laying across the overhead wires, blocking three tracks, with trackmen running towards me waving their arms and a red flag. I could do nothing but wait for my EMU to stop, by which time I had vacated the cab and moved into the small compartment at the rear. The EMU stopped with the front buried in the tree branches, then there was another ball of fire from the tree and the overhead wires, which were still live with 25,000 volts. The Spellbrook signalman had

placed all his signals at Danger, and now the overhead power was switched off. My guard and I then carried out our train protection duties. Although this incident may appear to have unfolded gradually, in actual fact it all happened in a matter of a few seconds. As you can imagine it was some time before services were back to normal.

I now received instructions to report to Stratford, as I was to have a conversion course to be trained on the 1,250hp Type 2/3 Brush diesel-electric locos. To start with there was the usual day in the classroom, then it was off to the diesel depot to get practical experience on the loco and learn all the 'faults and failures' that could occur. Towards the end of the week we were detailed to go 'light engine' to Liverpool Street and work a special train of four coaches to Albert Dock, the train being full of guests for a ship-naming ceremony at the docks. Driving the 1,250hp 'Toffee Apple' Brush to the docks was to be my practical test, our driver/instructor being fully conversant with the road. (The nickname 'Toffee Apple' arose from the shape of the controller handle fitted to the first of the class.)

'Toffee Apple' Brush Type 2/3 No 5503 (later Class 31) with an up freight leaving Hertford East in 1968.

On the approach to Stratford we were given the signal to take us round the curve and down to join the North Woolwich line just before Stratford Market and just past Stratford Low Level station. This part of the road was of great interest to me as it brought back many memories; the last time I had worked over it was as a fireman on an ex-GNR Class 'J52' during 1944/45. Passing Canning Town and Custom House and looking across to Victoria Docks it seemed unreal that nearly 20 years had passed since I had worked into that same dock. We were now almost at our destination, and arriving at Albert Dock, to the best of my recollection, we came under the supervision of the Port of London Authority. I never did find out which ship was being named, but we were not in the docks very long – the passengers alighted, then the shunters uncoupled our loco and off we went 'light engine' to Stratford depot, leaving our train at the docks. I had hoped that we might see the naming ceremony, but no such luck – nevertheless I enjoyed the trip, and I was now qualified to drive the 1,250hp Brush locos.

Then it was back to Hertford to work my rostered shifts on the EMUs and DMUs, as well as the diesel loco workings with parcel trains and loose-coupled freights, without incident – until one afternoon when I was working a three-car DMU down to Buntingford. Rounding a bend on the approach to Braughing, I was confronted by a cow standing in the middle of the track. I was travelling at approximately 50mph, and although I knew that it would be impossible to stop, I fully applied the brake and vacated the cab via the sliding door into the passenger section of the coach, where a passenger was looking horrified. After the inevitable impact the leading bogie was lifted up off the rail, then dropped back on, and eventually we stopped. The passenger said that he had travelled all the way from Kent for the ride to Buntingford, as he had heard rumours that the branch might close at some future date.

The guard and I examined the DMU for damage. The complete unit had passed over the cow, which was lying dead on the track some way to the rear of the unit. All the electrical and air connections between the coaches had been ripped apart, and some of the fuel pipes from the main fuel tank had also been ripped off, leaving diesel fuel gushing out onto the track with no means of shutting it off (the shut-off taps had also been broken off). I went back to see the passenger from Kent to tell him that I was sorry but he would not see Buntingford that day as our train was a complete failure. When the farmer who owned the animal arrived, he considered that I was to blame, and should have stopped to avoid hitting the animal! I will not go into the details of how the line was cleared except to say that no more trains ran over the Buntingford branch that afternoon or evening, and buses were brought in for the evening rush-hour.

One of our Saturday shifts was the 'Ware Shunt Pilot', which involved shunting the yard at Ware. It was a busy job, forming the train for the Temple Mills goods to pick up later in the day, and on completing the shunting we went 'light engine' to Hertford East, where the loco was stabled in a short siding near the MPD, as it would not be required until Monday morning.

Ware was a busy yard with various sidings, a coal yard and goods shed, and a rail connection with D. Wickham & Co, builders of diesel trains, railbuses and railway staff carriers that were exported all over the world. There was therefore enough work at Ware to justify a shunt pilot for an 8-hour shift, six days a week. The regular driver working here was a 'Green Card Man' who could work light duties only, and we covered the shift when he was either sick or on annual leave. I enjoyed working this shift as it was a break from the run to Liverpool Street with either an EMU or DMU.

As the existing loco on this working was to be replaced with a 204hp Drewry shunter, we had to be trained on it, and that meant another course. Some months later there was another change of loco, and we were then trained to drive a 165hp Ruston & Hornsby loco, which would be the final class of loco to work the yard at Ware.

At this period there was a great deal of freight working, with all the local yards busy, including those in the Lea Valley, and the up and down goods roads were well used between Temple Mills and Picketts Lock. There was also a named freight train, the 'Lea Valley Enterprise', which ran from Temple Mills to Whitemoor (March), picking up wagons as it worked its way north along the valley.

Working over the 'Bunt', as the Buntingford branch was known, was indeed a pleasure. The line was about 14 miles in length and passed through the beautiful Hertfordshire countryside; seeing it through all the different seasons of the year was a bonus. The station staff, signalmen and PW men were such a friendly lot to work with, and everyone knew each other. I suppose the best way to describe the branch is that it was run like a happy family, with everyone prepared to help each other if anything went wrong. With all my previous railway experience I had never worked over a line like it. There were bonuses at certain times of the year when we would get fresh fruit, soft fruit and vegetables – I even had the occasional pheasant.

Working the only freight train over the branch, which ran from Monday to Friday,

The Buntingford branch timetable for the summer of 1963.

was also a pleasure. After shunting the yard at St Margarets the first stop was Hadham, where the sidings were shunted, then Braughing yard was shunted. If we were within our schedule the signalman would make us a cup of tea, which we would enjoy in the hospitality of the signal box. Then it was off to Buntingford, where both the yard and the goods shed were shunted. Our only intermediate stop on the return trip was at Standon, where the flour mill sidings were shunted. Having completed that our next stop was the yard at St Margarets, where we left our train and went 'light engine' to Hertford, getting relieved on arrival.

In addition to the freight there was the DMU service, which only ran during the morning and evening rush-hour. I also enjoyed these workings, as very little went wrong. I have already mentioned the incident at Braughing with the cow, and

Exchanging the single-line staff at Braughing in 1962.

Above At the summit of the Buntingford branch on Hadham bank in 1962 with a Type 1 BTH Bo-Bo No D8209.

Below Inside Braughing signal box, 1962.

A lightweight St Margaret's freight at Buntingford in 1962.

sometimes sheep on the track could be a problem. One summer evening, while passing through Braughing Wood, I suddenly realised that a deer was trotting along the track ahead of me. I braked, and as I got nearer to the animal it suddenly leaped into the air, went over the fence and disappeared into the undergrowth – it amazed me to see how high these animals could jump. Then there was the odd scare when a farmer would drive a tractor and trailer across the track at a farm crossing as we were approaching, but I cannot recall any accidents. I must say that I enjoyed all of the work done on the 'Bunt'; the Rolls-Royce DMUs were ideal for the job, and both the NBL/GEC and BTH/Paxman locos were ideal for the freight

workings, although my personal choice would be the latter.

At about this period some of the BTH locos were fitted with two-way radios, so we could speak to a Control office, or they could contact us with instructions. This system had a very limited range and would not reach Buntingford, so it was back to the telephone system.

While on the subject of diesel locomotive workings, Hertford was allocated a diagram where we went passenger to Harlow Mill, relieved a Stratford crew, usually on a 1,365hp Brush, and spent several hours shunting the yard, being relieved by a March crew who would then work a train north, while we went passenger back to Hertford.

7
A TIME OF CHANGE

We are now into 1964, and there appeared to be signs of a decline in freight services generally – it was mentioned that at some future date all of the Lea Valley yards would be closed. In the meantime, because we were involved in freight movements at Bishops Stortford, Lea Valley and Temple Mills, I went on a course to be trained on the English Electric 1,750hp diesel locos (later Class 37), which meant yet another week at Stratford. The course took the usual pattern: theory in the classroom, faults and failures on the actual loco, then a practical test out on the road.

The latter proved to be interesting from my point of view, as it involved two of us driving a main-line train from Liverpool Street to King's Lynn. Although I knew most of the road to Cambridge, I had never been on the footplate from there to King's Lynn, but in the cab with us was a Loco Inspector and the actual driver, who was instructing us on the road and signals. I enjoyed this trip running over new metals and putting towns to names where I had never worked before. It was a glorious summer day, and it was good to handle a 1,750hp loco on this type of train. After a break at King's Lynn we worked the train back to Liverpool Street, where the Loco Inspector told us that we were now qualified to drive this class of loco. We made our way back to Hertford after a very interesting day out – and what made it better was the fact that we were getting paid for doing it.

Some weeks later we had some sad news. It had been decided by the powers that be to close the Buntingford branch for passenger traffic, but to retain it at this stage for freight. After the usual inquiries and public protests, which took several months, it was announced that the 'Bunt' would finally close to passenger trains on Saturday 14 November 1964. On that day I was working the first two trains over the branch; it was a typical November day with heavy cloud and the threat of rain. Both round trips were uneventful, except for the many passengers with their cameras who would be able to say that they went on the Buntingford branch on the last day of passenger train operation. Many of the regular passengers spoke to me to say that they were sorry to see the trains go, and that they had done their best to support the many protests and public meetings, but it had proved to be a lost cause – when the powers that be said something must close, they usually won!

For the next few months I would still be getting a few trips over the 'Bunt' on the goods working, although we knew there were plans to withdraw the freight services and, worst of all, lift the track. I enjoyed the few trips that were left working over the branch, but each one would be tinged with sadness. Eventually, on 17 September 1965, ten months after the last passenger train, the last freight train ran, picking up any wagons still standing in the yards and bringing them down to St Margarets. It was not long before engineering trains were picking up the track and recovering assets that might be of some future use as they worked south from Buntingford to St Margarets, worked by Stratford crews. Buffer stops were erected on part of the original branch beside the Hertford East line, which was used as a shunt spur for the yard at St Margarets.

The process of closing all the freight yards along the Lea Valley continued during the mid-1960s, with fewer and fewer freight trains using the old GE route from March to Temple Mills. To the best of my memory these trains were diverted via the GN main line, so that work could be carried out on the electrification of the Lea Valley line.

Over a long period while working the DMU service along the Lea Valley I was able to see lots of alterations taking place: the goods roads from Pickett's Lock southwards were lifted, many points, sidings and crossover points were removed, colour light signals replaced the old semaphores, with the equipment for carrying the overhead wires was installed, and while all this was going on we were still able to run a service. Signal boxes were demolished and stations rebuilt, so by the time the new electric service started during May 1969 the Lea Valley line was a new railway. Having driven DMUs for so many years along the Lea Valley, my first trip with a Class 305 EMU along the same tracks felt strange, but it all fell into place very quickly.

One of the things I had always dreaded was to have a fire on my train. One day I was working a Rolls-Royce DMU from Audley End to Liverpool Street – one of the objects of which was to pick up a train-load of pupils at Newport from the local grammar school for their journey home – and all went well until I ran into Sawbridgeworth station and the fire bell started ringing in my cab. Stopping, I looked back to find smoke rising from the last coach of my six-coach train (two three-car units).

All signals were put to danger on both the down and up lines by the Sawbridgeworth signalman, who could see the fire. When I reached the rear of the train the passengers were already on the platform, and my guard had already exhausted two fire extinguishers. We had by this time phoned for the fire

brigade, and had the overhead current switched off. Having used the two extinguishers I had taken from my cab, all we could do was wait for the fire engine. The fire had got a hold underneath with flames engulfing both the diesel engine and fuel tank – we had already operated the emergency fire equipment, but there appeared to be a defect. It was not very long before the fire brigade arrived and soon had the fire under control. As you can imagine, this incident had already shut down the Cambridge main line for a considerable time, and it was not all over yet, as a diesel loco came from Bishops Stortford to move our units into the down yard. Having done this, and before any trains could start running, both the track and the overhead electrics had to be checked.

Checking the interior of the damaged coach with the fire chief, he pointed to the large amount of homework papers on the floor and seats. His words to me were, 'When they go to school tomorrow they'll say, "Sorry, sir, no homework – the train caught fire on our way home."' Both my guard and myself then made our way to Cheshunt for the next part of our working, and to enjoy a well-earned meal break, pleased to leave our train at Sawbridgeworth. The next day the guard and I submitted a full report on the incident.

I must say that the assistance given to me by my guard was invaluable. There is now talk that in future years, with more modern trains, it will be a driver-only operation with no guard. Imagine having to cope with that situation without the help of a guard – it would be a nightmare!

One connection with the past that I saw every day was a steam locomotive working in the yard at Rye House Power Station. This loco worked there until the early 1970s, when progress caught up with it and it was replaced by an ex-BR diesel-mechanical shunter.

Being a member of the Hertford East branch of ASLEF I usually attended the branch meetings, which were held on a monthly basis. Having now been a member of the branch for some years I was asked to stand for nomination for our local Staff Representative Election. Our depot was allowed to have two reps, who were the

The Robert Stephenson & Hawthorn 0-6-0T that worked at Rye House Power Station, photographed in 1962. *Hertfordshire Mercury*

Chairman and Secretary, so to cut a long story short another driver and myself were elected. I became the Chairman, which involved attending meetings with the management and with all the Eastern Region reps. As we were representing all the drivers at our depot, we were also involved with the running of the depot, and having agreed to take this on I little realised how many years would be involved. There would be a little less train driving, as I would be doing some paperwork and attending meetings, but I must say I found it informative and interesting.

Over the years we attended meetings at Liverpool Street, King's Cross, Stratford, Cambridge, March, Doncaster, Bishops Stortford, Broxbourne, Enfield Town, Ilford depot and Southend, as well as some site meetings at various locations. From this description you might think that we had stopped driving trains, but we would sometimes go for weeks without a meeting, so there was still plenty of driving to be done.

There was one particular meeting of the Staff reps at Liverpool Street when we were informed that there was a serious health hazard in the cabs of the EMUs on which we were working in the form of blue asbestos, which was used as an insulation material between the inner section of the cab, and covered by the cab panelling. This created many problems, and after further meetings with the management and medical representatives it was agreed that all cabs would be sealed on the inner panelling pending removal of all the blue asbestos in a special building at Ilford depot. This meant that the destination indicators and head-codes could not be used, which created problems for the passengers over many months. In the event removal of the asbestos from the North East London (NEL) fleet of EMUs was to prove a mammoth task, but after a considerable length of time the units were classified as clean, and things got back to normal. At least the passengers now knew the destination of the train they were travelling on, and the signalman would be able to see the head-code.

There was the odd occasion when a little social life took place in the Hertford East staff room, which was long and narrow and thus perfect for a cine-film show. One midweek winter's evening those of us who were not working were privileged to see Bob Todd's films, which he made in about 1957 as an historic record of Great Eastern steam, showing the 'Jazz' lines in all their glory before electrification. Not only were the films very good, but Bob's commentary made the evening even more interesting. It is good to know that Bob had the foresight to film events that are now gone for ever.

In 1979 a different event took place at Hertford East, when, with a great deal of pomp Class 47 No 47172 was named *County of Hertfordshire*. Then, during the summer of 1984, to our surprise the Welsh Tourist Board

Special Train was stabled in the Hertford East yard for a week, so that the public could go and find out all about the attractions of Wales. To add interest to this event Talyllyn Railway loco *Sir Haydn* was stabled on a low-loader wagon in the station platform.

In the winter of 1985, out of the blue I received a phone call asking if I would assist in presenting an evening show on railways at Digswell Village Hall. Needless to say, the evening was a great success with an over-full hall, and was fully reported in the local paper.

Back to the summer of 1978, I was once again in the classroom at Ilford for a course on diesel-mechanical units, as these were to be used on Sundays over a long period due to extensive track works. Although I had been trained on these DMUs at King's Cross in 1959, the last time I had worked on one was early 1961. Only a few of us did the revision course, and after a week in the classroom we had nearly two weeks of instruction. Picking up an out-of-service DMU at Manningtree – used only for driver training purposes, and not carrying passengers – we worked it over the East Suffolk Line to Beccles, then, after a short break enjoying the local fish and chips, we worked it back to Manningtree. Once again I enjoyed working over lines that were new to me, and we were lucky to have a Driver/Instructor who made the course interesting.

Thinking back a few years, I recall working a Rolls-Royce DMU on a Sunday from Hertford East to Liverpool Street. Due to engineering work along part of the Lea Valley, I was diagrammed to take go via the Southbury Loop to Edmonton Junction, Lower Edmonton Low Level, Angel Road, Copper Mills Junction, Lea Bridge, Stratford and Liverpool Street. On arrival some alighting passengers asked me if I had been supplied with a map!

As the years slipped by many things changed at our depot. We were now only an EMU only, and worked on no other form of traction, which did tend to make the driver's job monotonous. Then the Diagram Office decided to introduce more flexibility – we were to learn the routes to Enfield Town, Chingford and Ilford EMU depot. This we welcomed, as it would give us more route knowledge and make our job less monotonous, as at present we sometimes worked three round trips from Hertford East to Liverpool Street, all stations along the Lea Valley then non-stop from Hackney Downs – making a total of 96 station stops, which does not take into account the large number of signal stops and other incidents. Over a five-day week this added up to 480 station stops.

Unfortunately during my career I was involved in three incidents with the overhead power lines being pulled down by my train. This was usually caused by a cantilever arm dropping down with the power line, which would foul the unit's pantograph, and at speed this would pull down the power line and could rip off the pantograph.

One of my worst experiences took place a short distance from Ware station travelling towards Liverpool Street. Without any warning there was a large bang with a blinding flash on the front of my unit (bear in mind that there are 25,000 volts in the overhead power line). I applied the emergency brake and stopped the train, then on inspection found that the overhead power cable was lying on the roof of the carriages, and the paint had been scorched on the front of the unit between the windscreens. I carried out the Rules & Regulations applicable to this emergency situation, being very thankful that the windscreens had not smashed. As you can imagine the line was shut for many hours.

On another occasion during the summer months I was standing in the platform at Broxbourne station at 04.00hrs, during a thunderstorm, when my unit was struck by lightning, which did a great deal of electrical damage, and the paint was scorched on the roof of the power car where the pantograph was located. I would like to say that it was very unlikely that any passengers would get electric shocks – if anything went wrong the main circuit-breakers tripped out at the main electrical supply depot.

Our Class 305 EMUs were soon to be replaced by a fleet of new Class 315s, so off we went again for a course to be trained on them. For this we travelled to Southend-on-Sea, where we had a intensive course and came to

Above A Class 310 EMU at Enfield Town on October 1987.

Right A new Class 315 unit at Hertford East in 1984.

the conclusion that the ultimate aim was that some time in the future there would be no train guards, as the units were designed for driver-only operation. When the train crews covering the North East London (NEL) area had been trained, all the Class 305 units were transferred away.

At about this time the trains to Bishops Stortford consisted of Class 312 EMUs, and we now had to be trained on those, involving a one-week course at Enfield Town.

Then there was the work on the reconstruction of Liverpool Street station, which took some years to complete. I saw much of this work being done, and it was amazing that a full normal service was operated, which said a great deal for the efficiency of the planners. I was told that it should be completed in 1991.

More changes came our way, the main one being our conditions of service. The management wanted to introduce continental

≈NSB≈	Adgangskort		Nr 09342
Navn og stilling Lok.fører R. Ruffell.		**Sted og datum** Had/Oslo 10/03.80.	
Adresse/Firma British Railways.		**Underskrift for NSB** *Ingv. Lund*	
Adgang til Lok's førerrum.		Jeg vedtar vilkårene på blankettens bakside om opphold på NSB's område	
Fra Åndalsnes til		**Innehaverens underskrift**	
Dombås.		*R. Ruffell*	
Ledsager(e)	**Gyldig i tiden** 21/07 02/08.80.	**Firmastempel og underskrift**	

80x50 sett. 12-75. H.C.

Bl. nr. 001.598.10

Left My footplate pass for the journey from Andalsnes to Dombas, 2 August 1980.

Below left Driver Olaf Danielsen in the cab of the General Motors diesel-electric loco at Dombas.

rostering, and at a meeting with them about the new proposed rosters it was explained that the working day would no longer be an 8-hour shift; for example, one day might be 6 hours, the next day 10 hours, then 8 hours, and so on. This would also involve starting a shift at a different time according to how the train diagram was worked out. At the end of the week the number of hours worked would still be 40 (five 8-hour days), but having done

shift-work all my working life it was only made tolerable by keeping the same shift for the week. We had one day off per week, which, working out over the weeks, was one day later each week, and this had worked well for years. As the depot's staff representatives we had many meetings with management about the new rosters, but in due course the new system was implemented. For example, a week's work might be as follows:

	On duty	Off duty
Sunday	22.00	06.00
Monday	18.00	02.00
Tuesday	14.00	22.00
Wednesday	Rest day	
Thursday	10.00	06.00
Friday	07.00	15.00
Saturday	05.00	13.00

This was a Rest Day Cover Week, and is not one of the better examples. The new shifts played havoc with eating and sleeping, as well as disorganising home and family life. I would add that I now found myself working out how long it would be before I could retire.

Travelling to Norway again in 1980, I had another interesting experience riding on the footplate from Andalsnes to Dombas, with Driver Olaf Danielsen. On my arrival at Andalsnes station a General Motors diesel-electric loco was already coupled on to the train. Driver Danielsen would be the driver to Dombas, a journey of 71 miles passing through magnificent mountain scenery, and he pointed out all the items of interest, including

Above The NSB loco and its train at Dombas; note the bars on the windscreen to protect the driver from falling ice and rocks.

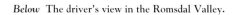

Below The driver's view in the Romsdal Valley.

Above On 27 July 1985 I travelled from King's Cross to Newcastle and return in the cab of an HST 125 along the as yet unelectrified East Coast Main Line. Crossing Stilton Fen we pass another HST heading south.

Below 120mph!

the metal bars in front of the windscreen to protect the loco from falling ice and rocks. All too soon we arrived at Dombas, where I changed trains to travel on to Oslo.

A further interesting trip was being invited to do the return trip from King's Cross to Newcastle in the cab of an HST 125 on 27 July 1985. This was an historic trip before the electrification north of Hitchin; also at that time all trains north went via Selby, as the main-line diversion round Selby to York had not yet been completed. Having been an East Coast fireman/driver for nearly 20 years, it was interesting to see how things had changed over the ensuing 24 years.

Many things had also changed during those years while I was working at Hertford East. Some sidings were clipped out of use, and overhead power lines were removed at Hertford East, which became unmanned between certain hours. Most freight using the GE line from March to Temple Mills now ran on the East Coast Main Line, and Temple Mills yard had partially closed. The up and down goods lines from Picketts Lock to Tottenham were lifted; Enfield Town MPD was closed in 1989 (having opened in 1845); and the connection from the GE line into Stansted Airport was under construction. Cameras and screens appeared at the ends of all stations on the NEL lines in preparation for driver-only operation, and EMUs were no longer stored at night in the few sidings that remained (originally there would have been about 12 units at night at Hertford East).

Subsequently I received a call to attend Ilford School for a course on radio telephones and driver-only operation, which was something I was not very happy about. Two of us from Hertford attended the course, with other drivers from different depots. It was obvious that all the responsibility of working a train would now be on the driver, and whatever might go wrong the driver would have to deal with it, without the back-up of a guard. With just under two years left to work, this did not appeal to me.

Because of the way our conditions of service had been eroded over the years, together with the monotony of constant EMU work, I had lost a great deal of interest in the job, so on 24 May 1982 I applied for a transfer to King's Cross. However, due to the way the transfer and redundancy system now worked, the only way I could move from Hertford was if I was made redundant, which at the time would be a very remote possibility. So there I was in early 1990 with nearly 48 years' service. I had often thought about taking early retirement, but that would mean retiring about 18 months before I become 65.

My wife and I had often discussed moving to North Yorkshire when I retired, as over the years we had spent a great deal of time in the North Yorkshire Moors area, and we also had relatives living near York. Then we had the chance of a new detached bungalow in North Yorkshire, in the area we wanted, so I applied for early retirement.

I retired on 28 July 1990 after completing 47 years and 49 weeks on the footplate. The last EMUs I drove were from Liverpool Street: a Class 312 unit to Broxbourne, where I was relieved, then I relieved on a 315 unit to Hertford East, where I was relieved by a Stratford driver. So, at the end of my career I shook hands with my guard at the unmanned Hertford East station, completed my daily work sheet, got into my car and drove home – not exactly an exciting finish to my long career.

However, it was a pleasant surprise a couple of weeks later when the Hertford East branch of ASLEF invited my wife and me to a retirement party in my honour. It was a memorable evening, and very much appreciated by both of us. There was a presentation for me, and a bouquet of flowers for my wife. It was a good send-off by my colleagues for our retirement, as three days later we would be moving to North Yorkshire.

Many people have asked me that, if I could go back and have my time again, would I still work on the railway. The answer is yes, because I enjoyed my first 20 years working on steam, and I was fortunate to have a long spell in the Top Link at Top Shed. I was also very fortunate to be rostered with good drivers, who passed on their knowledge to me, which stood me in good stead throughout my career. When the diesels came I found them interesting, but a lot of my enthusiasm had

gone. Then along came electric traction, for which I could not raise very much enthusiasm or interest. Every day's work was a repeat of the previous day with no variation, which was one of the biggest snags with working on nothing else but EMUs.

When steam finished many drivers and firemen left the railway and took other jobs in a variety of industries. I often wonder if what they did was the best thing, but as I have said I enjoyed my career until I became solely a EMU driver.

POSTSCRIPT

As I walked from my bungalow to Pickering station on the North Yorkshire Moors Railway on 13 June 1995, a glorious sunny afternoon, many things flashed through my mind about my footplate career on steam until I transferred from King's Cross to Hertford East. Today I had been invited by Geoff Morris, a NYMR driver, to have a footplate trip from Pickering to Grosmont and back, and when I arrived at the platform I was greeted by Geoff who invited me on to the footplate of BR Standard Class 4 No 75014.

To my surprise the loco was 'chimney north' (most tender locos work out of Pickering 'tender north'), but it had been turned ready to run 'light engine' to Scotland, as it was to do a spell of work on the West Highland Line between Fort William and Mallaig.

Return to the footplate: in the cab of BR Standard 4-6-0 No 75014 at Pickering on 13 June 1995.

Having not driven an 'A4' since 1960, it was a wonderful experience to re re-united with No 60007 *Sir Nigel Gresley* on the NYMR on 11 October 1996.

We now had a green light, and with the 'right away' from the guard Geoff opened the regulator and we started the 18-mile trip to Grosmont. On leaving Levisham I was invited by the fireman to have a go on the shovel, and found that I still had my firing skills, bearing in mind that I had been passed as a driver in June 1956, and that I had never worked as a fireman on any of the BR Standard classes – in fact, the only BR class I did a great deal of work on was the 9F 2-10-0, but as a driver. I enjoyed doing the firing, finding that No 75014 was a comfortable loco to work on, with instant results on the pressure gauge as soon as it was 'shown the shovel'.

The trip was full of interest, being on a class of loco I had never travelled on before. The line wound its way over the moors to Goathland, then it was a falling gradient to Grosmont, when the fireman could sit down. All too soon we passed the loco sheds, entered the tunnel and ran into Grosmont station.

We now ran round our train ready for the return trip to Pickering, which would be tender-first. I found the design of the tender a great asset for the crew, giving them full protection from the weather when running tender-first, somewhat different from some of the ex-GNR locos on which I had worked.

I enjoyed the trip back to Pickering, and it was great to be on the footplate of a steam loco after so many years. I would like to thank Geoff Morris and his fireman for making it such an enjoyable experience.

But that wasn't the end of it – Friday 11 October 1996 was to be my big day on the NYMR. Class 'A4' No 60007 *Sir Nigel Gresley* had been working on the line for nearly eight weeks, and I was invited to have a round trip on the footplate from Pickering to Grosmont.

On climbing on to the footplate I was again welcomed by Driver Geoff Morris and Fireman Steve Clark. Steve invited me to have a go on the shovel, so I did all of the firing to Grosmont without any effort, bearing in mind that I had not fired on an 'A4' for 40 years!

We had 1½ hours at Grosmont, so I was able to get busy with my camera, with very pleasing results. While there I was introduced to Roger Barker and other members of the A4 Society, which manages and owns *Sir Nigel Gresley*. I then made the fire up 'Northern fashion' for the return trip.

On leaving Grosmont Geoff, an ex-Midland (Derby) driver, invited me to take the regulator, saying that as I knew a great deal about the road, would I like to take the train to Pickering?

It was great to be back in the driving seat with the regulator wide open and cut-off at 45% climbing the 1 in 49 bank to Goathland, the Gresley three-cylinder beat sounding terrific! I couldn't believe it was me on the regulator – it seemed like a dream. Having enjoyed the trip I brought *Sir Nigel* to a halt in Pickering station.

Having not driven an 'A4' since 1960, this was for me a wonderful experience that I will never forget, getting the feel of an 'A4' again, particularly as it was one of those on which I had fired for thousands of miles during the 1950s, and had driven as a driver in my own right on odd occasions between 1956 and 1960.

Then on 30 October 1998 I had the privilege of a footplate trip on 'Schools' Class 4-4-0 *Repton*, and I must say I was impressed with the performance of the loco with 'six on' climbing the 1 in 49 bank from Grosmont to Goathland, especially as these locos had been built for the tracks of Kent.

The weather conditions were perfect with blue sky and sunshine as we left Pickering at 13.20. I did not do any driving, but sat and enjoyed the ride, watching other people doing the work. The forests and the moors looked beautiful in the late-afternoon sun, bringing out all the colours. There was no comfort in the cab – in fact, sitting on the fireman's seat my feet were perched on the two ratchet damper rods. I suppose running tender-first didn't help, but it was a good loco from a firing point of view.

We arrived at Grosmont with a layover of 2½ hours, which from my point of view was great. We shunted some stock around, filled the tank, posed the loco for photographs in the failing light, then backed on to our train ready to leave at 16.50. I did all of the firing coming back without any effort; it was a very good loco for a fireman, with pressure maintained at over the 200lb mark and just

I had, of course, never fired on or driven a Southern Railway 'Schools' Class 4-4-0, so was pleased when I managed to keep 'top side' of No 30926 *Repton* on the NYMR on 30 October 1998.

over half a glass of water. As we left Grosmont it was getting dark, with the moon climbing into the sky, so I fired the loco all the way back to Pickering in moonlight. This brought back many memories, with the glare from the firebox lighting up the sky and hillsides, and the moonlight showing up the rails and shining on the boiler as we went through Newtondale. The moon reflecting from our exhaust was very impressive, and we arrived at Pickering after a very good trip. I was complemented by Geoff Morris on my firing; he said that many BR firemen would have liked to have finished their trip with a perfect fire like mine!

I enjoyed every minute of that memorable trip – even at my age I was able to keep 'top side' of a loco that I had never even set foot on before.

Finally, Geoff Morris again kindly invited me to have another footplate trip on the NYMR on 21 October 1999. There was heavy cloud with a few spots of rain in the air, which

was not a very good omen for running 18 miles tender-first. The 11.20 train was in the platform with BR Standard 2-6-4T No 80135 simmering at the safety valves, and I was welcomed on to the footplate by Geoff, who introduced me to Allan, his fireman. It was good to be on this loco for two main reasons: first, I had never been on one before, and second, we would be running 'bunker-first', which would be a great advantage over tender-first running in the poor weather conditions.

On this trip I did no firing, but sat and enjoyed the ride through the forests and over the moors with all the autumn colours. The loco performance was very impressive, and in my opinion it was a comfortable loco to work on, far superior to the Thompson Class 'L1' 2-6-4Ts on which I had worked out of King's Cross.

On our arrival at Grosmont we were relieved by another crew, giving us 2½ hours to have a coffee and a sandwich, then off we

On 21 October 1999 it was great to be back in the driving seat again, this time on 'K1' 2-6-0 No 62005. The 'K1' was ideal for the hilly NYMR, and the bark of the exhaust reminded me of firing and driving 'B1' 4-6-0s well over 40 years before.

went to Grosmont shed, where I was introduced to the Shed Foreman and Keith Gays, the Chief Locomotive Inspector (Geoff Morris is also a Loco Inspector). We had a walk round the workshops, then went into the running shed where 'A4' *Sir Nigel Gresley* and 'V2' *Green Arrow* were on the same road, reminding me of my days at Top Shed. We then went into the MIC classroom, which was very well equipped with working models of valve gears, etc, and instructional data; here the line's future fireman and drivers would gain their knowledge.

We then made our way back to Grosmont station to work the 14.50 train back to Pickering with Thompson Class 'K1' 2-6-0 No 62005. By now it was pouring with rain, with low cloud and mist, and as we left Grosmont our loco did a couple of slips, then found her feet and we were away. Geoff then came over to me, saying, 'You know where all the bits are – take her back to Pickering.'

Of course I was delighted – it was great to be in the driving seat again, enjoying the 1 in 49 climb up the bank to Goathland. The 'K1' was ideal for this road, with its smaller wheels, and it was in very good condition. The bark at the chimney top sounded great, reminding me of the work I had done both as a fireman and driver on the Class 'B1' 4-6-0s well over 40 years before.

Waiting for the 'right away' I had a problem seeing the guard due to the steam heating on the train obscuring parts of the platform (another memory), but having got 'right away' I released the brakes, opened the regulator and off we went, finishing the climb up the bank. Having got over the summit I 'wound her up' (reduced the cut-off) and eased the regulator; with the chimney exhaust reduced I found that the weather conditions were so bad that the exhaust was coming down along the boiler, obscuring my vision (another memory). There was no one to pick up at Newtondale Halt, so our next stop was Levisham, where the token was changed. We then continued through the forest and I brought No 62005 to a stop at Pickering station. Once again it was thanks to Geoff for an unforgettable day out, one that brought back many memories.

APPENDIX
LOCOS, LINES AND DEPOTS ENCOUNTERED, 1942–90

LOCOMOTIVE DEPOTS INVOLVED WITH AS A FIREMAN

King's Cross ('Top Shed')
Hornsey
Hatfield
Hitchin
Cambridge
Peterborough (New England)
Grantham
Retford
York
Newcastle (Gateshead)
Edinburgh (Haymarket)
Leeds (Copley Hill and Neville Hill)
Neasden
Feltham and Hither Green (Southern Region)

LOCOMOTIVES WORKED ON AS A FIREMAN

Ex-LNER

0-6-0	'J6', 'J11', 'J15', 'J17', 'J39'
2-6-0	'K1', 'K2', 'K3'
2-6-2	'V2'
2-8-0	'O1', 'O2', 'O4'
2-8-2	'P1'
4-4-0	'D2', 'D16'
4-4-2	'C1'
4-6-0	'B1', 'B2', 'B17'
4-6-2	'A1' ('A10'), 'A1', 'A2/1', 'A2/2', 'A2/3', 'A3', 'A4'
4-6-4	'W1'
4-6-2T	'A5'
4-4-2T	'C12'
2-4-2T	'F2'
0-6-0T	'J50'
0-6-0ST	'J52'
2-6-4T	'L1'
0-6-2T	'N1', 'N2', 'N7'

Ex-LMS

2-8-0	8F

War Department

2-8-0, 2-10-0

ROUTES WORKED OVER AS A FIREMAN FROM KING'S CROSS

All local freight and suburban/empty coach workings (as at Hornsey depot)
Finsbury Park to Broad Street, Moorgate, Alexandra Palace, Mill Hill East, Edgware, High Barnet, Highgate (London Transport sidings)
King's Cross to Cambridge via Hitchin
King's Cross to Leeds and Newcastle via Doncaster
King's Cross to Skegness via Spalding, Boston and Firsby
King's Cross to Doncaster via Spalding, Sleaford, Lincoln and Gainsborough

Doncaster to York via Knottingley

York to Darlington via Knaresborough, Ripon and Northallerton

Darlington to Newcastle via Bishop Auckland

Darlington to Newcastle via Sunderland

Leeds to Doncaster via Wakefield and Knottingley

Leeds to Doncaster via Wakefield

King's Cross to Edinburgh (as a passenger from Tollerton to Edinburgh on the non-stop)

Hertford North to Welwyn Garden City (passenger service withdrawn 18 June 1951)

Places worked to as a driver based at Top Shed

King's Cross (passenger) to Doncaster

King's Cross (passenger) to Hitchin via Hertford North

King's Cross (passenger) to Cambridge via Hitchin

Holloway Carriage Sidings, Western Sidings, Waterworks Sidings, Bounds Green, Hornsey Carriage Sidings, Finsbury Park Carriage Sidings

King's Cross (goods) to Clarence Yard, East Goods Yard, Highbury Vale, Ashburton Grove, Holloway Cattle Dock, Ferme Park

Highbury Vale to Mill Hill East, Edgware, High Barnet, Highgate Sidings (LT)

Finsbury Park to Broad Street and Moorgate

All King's Cross Goods Yard workings including North London Line transfer sidings and the sidings for Rowntrees on the down side just above Copenhagen Tunnel

Routes worked over while at Hertford East MPD

St Margarets to Buntingford

Liverpool Street to Audley End, Enfield Town, Hertford East, Chingford, Ilford

EMU depot and Tottenham Hale via Stratford

Southbury branch

Lea Valley line

Temple Mills Yard and MPD

Stratford MPD

Billet DMU Sidings, High Meads, Stratford

Edmonton Junction to Angel Road

Routes worked over with a conductor/driver

Ilford to Southend-on-Sea

Stratford to Albert Dock

Audley End to King's Lynn

Manningtree to Ipswich and Beccles via the East Suffolk Line

Seven Sisters to Coppermills Junction via South Tottenham

Complete summary of diesel locos, DMUs and EMUs qualified to drive

Locomotives

1956 TOPS Classes 08 and 09 shunters (350hp): English Electric, BTH/Blackstone, GEC/Blackstone. 350HP

1959 Type 2: NBL/Mann (1,000hp), Birmingham C&W/Sulzer (1,160hp)

1960 Type 2: Brush/Mirrlees (1,365hp)

1962 Type 1: BTH/Paxman (800hp); TOPS Class 01 (153hp): Andrew Barclay

1963 Type 1: NBL/GEC (800hp), Brush/Mirrlees (1,250hp)

1964 Type 3: English Electric (1,750hp); TOPS Class 03 (204hp): Drewry

1965 Ruston & Hornsby (165hp)

DMUs

1959 Craven (500hp)

1961 Rolls-Royce (Derby) (1,000hp)

EMUs

1961-87 English Electric and General Electric Classes 302, 304, 305, 308, 310, 315

INDEX